POCKET GUIDE
TO THE

ADA

Americans with
Disabilities Act
**Accessibility Guidelines
for Buildings and Facilities**

Revised Edition

Evan Terry Associates, P.C.

John Wiley & Sons, Inc.
New York • Chichester • Weinheim • Brisbane •
Singapore • Toronto

DISCARD

COMPILED and © 1997 by
EVAN TERRY ASSOCIATES, P.C.
BIRMINGHAM, AL
(205) 972-9101 (voice), (205) 972-9112 (TDD)
& (205) 972-9110 (fax)

Published by John Wiley & Sons, Inc.

Library of Congress Cataloging-in-Publication Data

Pocket guide to the ADA : Americans with Disabilities Act
   accessibility guidelines for buildings and facilities / Evan Terry
   Associates. -- Rev. ed.
      p. cm.
   Rev. ed. of : Pocket guide to the Americans with Disabilities Act
accessibility guidelines for buildings and facilities. c1993.
   Includes index.
   ISBN: 0-471-18137-4 (paper : alk. paper)
   1. Architecture and the physically handicapped--Law and
legislation--United States. I. Evan Terry Associates, P.C.
II. Pocket guide to the Americans with Disabilities Act
accessibility guidelines for buildings and facilities.
KF5709.3.H35P63   1997   97-1549

Printed in the United States of America

10 9 8 7 6 5 4 3

NOTE TO READERS

This publication has been compiled from the Americans with Disabilities Act Accessibility Guidelines for Buildings and Facilities, Appendix A to the Department of Justice ("DOJ") Regulations printed in the Federal Register, Vol. 56, No. 144, July 26, 1991 and Appendix A to Part 37 - Standards for Accessible Transportation Facilities printed in the Federal Register, Vol. 56, No 173, September 6, 1991 and the following amendments (noted by sidebars in the text):
1. Sections 4.30.4 and 7.3(1) - Technical Corrections (April 5, 1993);
2. Sections 10.3.1(7), 4.1.3(20), 4.34.1 - 4.34.5 - Fare Vending Machine Reach Ranges (July 15, 1993);
3. Sections 10.3.1, 10.3.1(7) and 10.3.2 - Final Rule-Miscellaneous Changes (Nov. 30, 1993);
4. Section 10 - Transportation Facilities (Jan. 18, 1994);
5. Sections 4.1.3(20), 4.34.1 - 4.34.5, 10.3.1(7) - ATM Reach Ranges, Transportation Facilities (Jan. 18, 1994);
6. Sections 4.7.7, 4.29.5, 4.29.6 - Detectable Warnings Suspension (April 12, 1994);
7. Sections 4.7.7, 4.29.5, 4.29.6 - Extension of Detectable Warnings Suspension (July 29, 1996).

Copies of these documents may be obtained by contacting one of the following:
The Disabilities Rights Section, Civil Rights Division
U.S. Department of Justice
P.O. Box 66738, Washington, DC 20035-6738
(800) 514-0301(voice) or (800) 514-0383 (TTY);
The U. S. Architectural and Transportation Barriers Compliance Board (ATBCB)
Suite 1000, 1331 F Street NW, Washington, DC 20004-1111
(800) 872-2253 (voice) or (800) 993-2822 (TTY); or
The U. S. Department of Transportation ("DOT"),
400 7th Street NW, Room 10424, Washington, DC 20590
(202) 366-1656 (voice) or (202) 366-4567 (TTY).

UPCOMING CHANGES
As the ATBCB revises the ADA Guidelines for Buildings and Facilities and those changes and new sections are adopted by DOJ as ADA Design Standards, the Pocket Guide to the ADAAG will be updated to reflect those changes. **If you would like notice of those updates** contact us at (205) 972-9101 (voice), (205) 972-9112 (TTY) & (205) 972-9110 (fax).

TABLE OF CONTENTS

1. Purpose.
This document sets guidelines for accessibility to places of public accommodation and commercial facilities by individuals with disabilities. These guidelines are to be applied during the design, construction, and alteration of such buildings and facilities to the extent required by regulations issued by Federal agencies, including the Department of Justice, under the Americans with Disabilities Act of 1990.

The technical specifications 4.2 through 4.35, of these guidelines are the same as those of the American National Standard Institute's document A117.1-1980. [ETA Editor's note: Since this Pocket Guide to ADAAG is printed in reduced size fonts, all italics have been omitted for clarity.] However, sections 4.1.1 through 4.1.7 and sections 5 through 10 are different from ANSI A117.1 in their entirety and are printed in standard type.

The illustrations and text of ANSI A117.1 are reproduced with permission from the American National Standards Institute. Copies of the standard may be purchased from the American National Standards Institute at 1430 Broadway, New York, New York 10018.

2. General

2.1 Provisions for Adults. The specifications in these guidelines are based upon adult dimensions and anthropometrics.

2.2* Equivalent Facilitation. Departures from particular technical and scoping requirements of this guideline by the use of other designs and technologies are permitted where the alternative designs and technologies used will provide substantially equivalent or greater access to and usability of the facility.

3. Miscellaneous Instructions and Definitions.

3.1 Graphic Conventions. Graphic conventions are shown in Table 1. Dimensions that are not marked minimum or maximum are absolute, unless otherwise indicated in the text or captions.

3.2 Dimensional Tolerances. All dimensions are subject to conventional building industry tolerances for field conditions.

3.3 Notes. The text of these guidelines does not contain notes or footnotes. Additional information, explanations, and advisory materials are located in the Appendix. Paragraphs marked with an asterisk have related, non-mandatory material in the Appendix. In the Appendix, the corresponding paragraph numbers are preceded by an A.

3.4 General Terminology.

comply with. Meet one or more specifications of these guidelines.

if, if ... then. Denotes a specification that applies only when the conditions described are present.

may. Denotes an option or alternative.

shall. Denotes a mandatory specification or requirement.

should. Denotes an advisory specification or recommendation.

3.5 Definitions.

Access Aisle. An accessible pedestrian space between elements, such as parking spaces, seating, and desks, that provides clearances appropriate for use of the elements.

Accessible. Describes a site, building, facility, or portion thereof that complies with these guidelines.

Accessible Element. An element specified by these guidelines (for example, telephone, controls, and the like).

Accessible Route. A continuous unobstructed path connecting all accessible elements and spaces of a building or facility. Interior accessible routes may include corridors, floors, ramps, elevators, lifts, and clear floor space at fixtures. Exterior accessible routes may include parking access aisles, curb ramps, crosswalks at vehicular ways, walks, ramps, and lifts.

Accessible Space. Space that complies with these guidelines.

Adaptability. The ability of certain building spaces and elements, such as kitchen counters, sinks, and grab bars, to be added or altered so as to accommodate the needs of individuals with or without disabilities or to accommodate the needs of persons with different types or degrees of disability.

Addition. An expansion, extension, or increase in the gross floor area of a building or facility.

Administrative Authority. A governmental agency that adopts or enforces regulations and guidelines for the design, construction, or alteration of buildings and facilities.

Alteration. An alteration is a change to a building or facility made by, on behalf of, or for the use of a public accommodation or commercial facility, that affects or could affect the usability of the building or facility or part thereof. Alterations include, but are not limited to, remodeling, renovation, rehabilitation, reconstruction, historic restoration, changes or rearrangement of the structural parts or elements, and changes or rearrangement in the plan configuration of walls and full-height partitions. Normal maintenance, reroofing, painting or wallpapering, or changes to mechanical and electrical systems are not alterations unless they affect the usability of the building or facility.

Area of Rescue Assistance. An area, which has direct access to an exit, where people who are unable to use stairs may remain temporarily in safety to await further instructions or assistance during emergency evacuation.

Assembly Area. A room or space accommodating a group of individuals for recreational, educational, political, social, or amusement purposes, or for the consumption of food and drink.

Automatic Door. A door equipped with a power-operated mechanism and controls that open and close the door automatically upon receipt of a momentary actuating signal. The switch that begins the automatic cycle may be a photoelectric device, floor mat, or manual switch (see power-assisted door).

Building. Any structure used and intended for supporting or sheltering any use or occupancy.

Circulation Path. An exterior or interior way of passage from one place to another for pedestrians, including, but not limited to, walks, hallways, courtyards, stairways, and stair landings.

Clear. Unobstructed.

Clear Floor Space. The minimum unobstructed floor or ground space required to accommodate a single, stationary wheelchair and occupant.

Closed Circuit Telephone. A telephone with dedicated line(s) such as a house phone, courtesy phone or phone that must be used to gain entrance to a facility.

Common Use. Refers to those interior and exterior rooms, spaces, or elements that are made available for the use of a restricted group of people (for example, occupants of a homeless shelter, the occupants of an office building, or the guests of such occupants).

Cross Slope. The slope that is perpendicular to the direction of travel (see running slope).

Curb Ramp. A short ramp cutting through a curb or built up to it.

Detectable Warning. A standardized surface feature built in or applied to walking surfaces or other elements to warn visually impaired people of hazards on a circulation path.

Dwelling Unit. A single unit which provides a kitchen or food preparation area, in addition to rooms and spaces for living, bathing, sleeping, and the like. Dwelling units include a single family home or a townhouse used as a transient group home; an apartment building used as a shelter; guestrooms in a hotel that provide sleeping accommodations and food preparation areas; and other similar facilities used on a transient basis. For purposes of these guidelines, use of the term "Dwelling Unit" does not imply the unit is used as a residence.

Egress, Means of. A continuous and unobstructed way of exit travel from any point in a building or facility to a public way. A means of egress comprises vertical and horizontal travel and may include intervening room spaces, doorways, hallways, corridors, passageways, balconies, ramps, stairs, enclosures, lobbies, horizontal exits, courts and yards. An accessible means of egress is one that complies with these guidelines and does not include stairs, steps, or escalators. Areas of rescue assistance or evacuation elevators may be included as part of accessible means of egress.

Element. An architectural or mechanical component of a building, facility, space, or site, e.g., telephone, curb ramp, door, drinking fountain, seating, or water closet.

Entrance. Any access point to a building or portion of a building or facility used for the purpose of entering. An entrance includes the approach walk, the vertical access leading to the entrance platform, the entrance platform itself, vestibules if provided, the entry door(s) or gate(s), and the hardware of the entry door(s) or gate(s).

Facility. All or any portion of buildings, structures, site improvements, complexes, equipment, roads, walks, passageways, parking lots, or other real or personal property located on a site.

Ground Floor. Any occupiable floor less than one story above or below grade with direct access to grade. A building or facility always has at least one ground floor and may have more than one ground floor as where a split level entrance has been provided or where a building is built into a hillside.

Mezzanine or Mezzanine Floor. That portion of a story which is an intermediate floor level placed within the story and having occupiable space above and below its floor.

Marked Crossing. A crosswalk or other identified path intended for pedestrian use in crossing a vehicular way.

Multifamily Dwelling. Any building containing more than two dwelling units.

Occupiable. A room or enclosed space designed for human occupancy in which individuals congregate for amusement, educational or similar purposes, or in which occupants are engaged at labor, and which is equipped with means of egress, light, and ventilation.

Operable Part. A part of a piece of equipment or appliance used to insert or withdraw objects, or to activate, deactivate, or adjust the equipment or appliance (for example, coin slot, push-button, handle).

Path of Travel. (Reserved).

Power-assisted Door. A door used for human passage with a mechanism that helps to open the door, or relieves the opening resistance of a door, upon the activation of a switch or a continued force applied to the door itself.

Public Use. Describes interior or exterior rooms or spaces that are made available to the general public. Public use may be provided at a building or facility that is privately or publicly owned.

Ramp. A walking surface which has a running slope greater than 1:20.

Running Slope. The slope that is parallel to the direction of travel (see cross slope).

Service Entrance. An entrance intended primarily for delivery of goods or services.

Signage. Displayed verbal, symbolic, tactile, and pictorial information.

Site. A parcel of land bounded by a property line or a designated portion of a public right-of-way.

Site Improvement. Landscaping, paving for pedestrian and vehicular ways, outdoor lighting, recreational facilities, and the like, added to a site.

Sleeping Accommodations. Rooms in which people sleep; for example, dormitory and hotel or motel guest rooms or suites.

Space. A definable area, e.g., room, toilet room, hall, assembly area, entrance, storage room, alcove, courtyard, or lobby.

Story. That portion of a building included between the upper surface of a floor and upper surface of the floor or roof next above. If such portion of a building does not include occupiable space, it is not considered a story for purposes of these guidelines. There may be more than one floor level within a story as in the case of a mezzanine or mezzanines.

Structural Frame. The structural frame shall be considered to be the columns and the girders, beams, trusses and spandrels having direct connections to the columns and all other members which are essential to the stability of the building as a whole.

Tactile. Describes an object that can be perceived using the sense of touch.

Text Telephone. Machinery or equipment that employs interactive graphic (i.e., typed) communications through the transmission of coded signals across the standard telephone network. Text telephones can include, for example, devices known as TDD's (telecommunication display devices or telecommunication devices for deaf persons) or computers.

Transient Lodging. A building, facility, or portion thereof, excluding inpatient medical care facilities, that contains one or more dwelling units or sleeping accommodations. Transient lodging may include, but is not limited to, resorts, group homes, hotels, motels, and dormitories.

Vehicular Way. A route intended for vehicular traffic, such as a street, driveway, or parking lot.

Walk. An exterior pathway with a prepared surface intended for pedestrian use, including general pedestrian areas such as plazas and courts.

NOTE: Sections 4.1.1 through 4.1.7 are different from ANSI A117.1 in their entirety and are printed in standard type (ANSI A117.1 does not include scoping provisions).

4. ACCESSIBLE ELEMENTS AND SPACES: SCOPE AND TECHNICAL REQUIREMENTS.

4.1 Minimum Requirements

4.1.1* Application.

(1) General. All areas of newly designed or newly constructed buildings and facilities required to be accessible by 4.1.2 and 4.1.3 and altered portions of existing buildings and facilities required to be accessible by 4.1.6 shall comply with these guidelines, 4.1 through 4.35, unless otherwise provided in this section or as modified in a special application section.

(2) Application Based on Building Use. Special application sections 5 through 10 provide additional requirements for restaurants and cafeterias, medical care facilities, business and mercantile, libraries, accessible transient lodging, and transportation facilities. When a building or facility contains more than one use covered by a special application section, each portion shall comply with the requirements for that use.

(3)* Areas Used Only by Employees as Work Areas. Areas that are used only as work areas shall be designed and constructed so that individuals with disabilities can approach, enter, and exit the areas. These guidelines do not require that any areas used only as work areas be constructed to permit maneuvering within the work area or be constructed or equipped (i.e., with racks or shelves) to be accessible.

(4) Temporary Structures. These guidelines cover temporary buildings or facilities as well as permanent facilities. Temporary buildings and facilities are not of permanent construction but are extensively used or are essential for public use for a period of time. Examples of temporary buildings or facilities covered by these guidelines include, but are not limited to: reviewing stands, temporary classrooms, bleacher areas, exhibit areas, temporary banking facilities, temporary health screening services, or temporary safe pedestrian passageways around a construction site. Structures, sites and equipment directly associated with the actual processes of construction, such as scaffolding, bridging, materials hoists, or construction trailers are not included.

(5) General Exceptions.

(a) In new construction, a person or entity is not required to meet fully the requirements of these guidelines where that person or entity can demonstrate that it is structurally impracticable to do so. Full compliance will be considered structurally impracticable only in those rare circumstances when the unique characteristics of terrain prevent the incorporation of accessibility features. If full compliance with the requirements of these guidelines is structurally impracticable, a person or entity shall comply with the requirements to the extent it is not structurally impracticable. Any portion of the building or facility which can be made accessible shall comply to the extent that it is not structurally impracticable.

(b) Accessibility is not required to (i) observation galleries used primarily for security purposes; or (ii) in non-occupiable spaces accessed only by ladders, catwalks, crawl spaces, very narrow passageways, or freight (non-passenger) elevators, and frequented only by service personnel for repair purposes; such spaces include, but are not limited to, elevator pits, elevator penthouses, piping or equipment catwalks.

4.1.2 Accessible Sites and Exterior Facilities: New Construction.

An accessible site shall meet the following minimum requirements:

(1) At least one accessible route complying with 4.3 shall be provided within the boundary of the site from public transportation stops, accessible parking spaces, passenger loading zones if provided, and public streets or sidewalks, to an accessible building entrance.

(2) At least one accessible route complying with 4.3 shall connect accessible buildings, accessible facilities, accessible elements, and accessible spaces that are on the same site.

(3) All objects that protrude from surfaces or posts into circulation paths shall comply with 4.4.

(4) Ground surfaces along accessible routes and in accessible spaces shall comply with 4.5.

(5) (a) If parking spaces are provided for self-parking by employees or visitors, or both, then accessible spaces complying with 4.6 shall be provided in each such parking area in conformance with the table below. Spaces required by the table need not be provided in the particular lot. They may be provided in a different location if equivalent or greater accessibility, in terms of distance from an accessible entrance, cost and convenience is ensured.

TOTAL PARKING IN LOT	REQUIRED MINIMUM NUMBER OF ACCESSIBLE SPACES
1 to 25	1
26 to 50	2
51 to 75	3
76 to 100	4
101 to 150	5
151 to 200	6
201 to 300	7
301 to 400	8
401 to 500	9
501 to 1000	2 percent of total
1001 and over	20, plus 1 for each 100 over 1000

Except as provided in (b), access aisles adjacent to accessible spaces shall be 60 in (1525 mm) wide minimum.

(b) One in every eight accessible spaces, but not less than one, shall be served by an access aisle 96 in (2440 mm) wide minimum and shall be designated "van accessible" as required by 4.6.4. The vertical clearance at such spaces shall comply with 4.6.5. All such spaces may be grouped on one level of a parking structure.

EXCEPTION: Provision of all required parking spaces in conformance with "Universal Parking Design" (see appendix A4.6.3) is permitted.

(c) If passenger loading zones are provided, then at least one passenger loading zone shall comply with 4.6.6.

(d) At facilities providing medical care and other services for persons with mobility impairments, parking spaces complying with 4.6 shall be provided in accordance with 4.1.2(5)(a) except as follows:

(i) Outpatient units and facilities: 10 percent of the total number of parking spaces provided serving each such outpatient unit or facility;

(ii) Units and facilities that specialize in treatment or services for persons with mobility impairments: 20 percent of the total number of parking spaces provided serving each such unit or facility.

(e)* Valet parking: Valet parking facilities shall provide a passenger loading zone complying with 4.6.6 located on an accessible route to the entrance of the facility. Paragraphs 5(a), 5(b), and 5(d) of this section do not apply to valet parking facilities.

(6) If toilet facilities are provided on a site, then each such public or common use toilet facility shall comply with 4.22. If bathing facilities are provided on a site, then each such public or common use bathing facility shall comply with 4.23.

For single user portable toilet or bathing units clustered at a single location, at least 5% but no less than one toilet unit or bathing unit complying with 4.22 or 4.23 shall be installed at each cluster whenever typical inaccessible units are provided. Accessible units shall be identified by the International Symbol of Accessibility.

EXCEPTION: Portable toilet units at construction sites used exclusively by construction personnel are not required to comply with 4.1.2(6).

(7) Building Signage. Signs which designate permanent rooms and spaces shall comply with 4.30.1, 4.30.4, 4.30.5 and 4.30.6. Other signs which provide direction to, or information about, functional spaces of the building shall comply with 4.30.1, 4.30.2, 4.30.3, and 4.30.5. Elements and spaces of accessible facilities which shall be identified by the International Symbol of Accessibility and which shall comply with 4.30.7 are:

(a) Parking spaces designated as reserved for individuals with disabilities;

(b) Accessible passenger loading zones;

(c) Accessible entrances when not all are accessible (inaccessible entrances shall have directional signage to indicate the route to the nearest accessible entrance);

(d) Accessible toilet and bathing facilities when not all are accessible.

4.1.3 Accessible Buildings: New Construction. Accessible buildings and facilities shall meet the following minimum requirements:

(1) At least one accessible route complying with 4.3 shall connect accessible building or facility entrances with all accessible spaces and elements within the building or facility.

(2) All objects that overhang or protrude into circulation paths shall comply with 4.4.

(3) Ground and floor surfaces along accessible routes and in accessible rooms and spaces shall comply with 4.5.

(4) Interior and exterior stairs connecting levels that are not connected by an elevator, ramp, or other accessible means of vertical access shall comply with 4.9.

(5)* One passenger elevator complying with 4.10 shall serve each level, including mezzanines, in all multi-story buildings and facilities unless exempted below. If more than one elevator is provided, each full passenger elevator shall comply with 4.10.

EXCEPTION 1: Elevators are not required in facilities that are less than three stories or that have less than 3000 square feet per story unless the building is a shopping center, a shopping mall, or the professional office of a health care provider, or another type of facility as determined by the Attorney General. The elevator exemption set forth in this paragraph does not obviate or limit in any way the obligation to comply with the other accessibility requirements established in section 4.1.3. For example, floors above or below the accessible ground floor must meet the requirements of this section except for elevator service. If toilet or bathing facilities are provided on a level not served by an elevator, then toilet or bathing facilities must be provided on the accessible ground floor. In new construction if a building or facility is eligible for this exemption but a full passenger elevator is nonetheless planned, that elevator shall meet the requirements of 4.10 and shall serve each level in the building. A full passenger elevator that provides service from a garage to only one level of a building or facility is not required to serve other levels.

EXCEPTION 2: Elevator pits, elevator penthouses, mechanical rooms, piping or equipment catwalks are exempted from this requirement.

EXCEPTION 3: Accessible ramps complying with 4.8 may be used in lieu of an elevator.

EXCEPTION 4: Platform lifts (wheelchair lifts) complying with 4.11 of this guideline and applicable state or local codes may be used in lieu of an elevator only under the following conditions:

(a) To provide an accessible route to a performing area in an assembly occupancy.

(b) To comply with the wheelchair viewing position line-of-sight and dispersion requirements of 4.33.3.

(c) To provide access to incidental occupiable spaces and rooms which are not open to the general public and which house no more than five persons, including but not limited to equipment control rooms and projection booths.

(d) To provide access where existing site constraints or other constraints make use of a ramp or an elevator infeasible.

(6) Windows: (Reserved).

(7) Doors:

(a) At each accessible entrance to a building or facility, at least one door shall comply with 4.13.

(b) Within a building or facility, at least one door at each accessible space shall comply with 4.13.

(c) Each door that is an element of an accessible route shall comply with 4.13.

(d) Each door required by 4.3.10, Egress, shall comply with 4.13.

(8) In new construction, at a minimum, the requirements in (a) and (b) below shall be satisfied independently:

(a)   (i) At least 50% of all public entrances (excluding those in (b) below) must be accessible. At least one must be a ground floor entrance. Public entrances are any entrances that are not loading or service entrances.

     (ii) Accessible entrances must be provided in a number at least equivalent to the number of exits required by the applicable building/fire codes. (This paragraph does not require an increase in the total number of entrances planned for a facility.)

     (iii) An accessible entrance must be provided to each tenancy in a facility (for example, individual stores in a strip shopping center).

One entrance may be considered as meeting more than one of the requirements in (a). Where feasible, accessible entrances shall be the entrances used by the majority of people visiting or working in the building.

(b)   (i) In addition, if direct access is provided for pedestrians from an enclosed parking garage to the building, at least one direct entrance from the garage to the building must be accessible.

     (ii) If access is provided for pedestrians from a pedestrian tunnel or elevated walkway, one entrance to the building from each tunnel or walkway must be accessible.

One entrance may be considered as meeting more than one of the requirements in (b).

Because entrances also serve as emergency exits whose proximity to all parts of buildings and facilities is accessible.

(c) If the only entrance to a building, or tenancy in a facility, is a service entrance, that entrance shall be accessible.

(d) Entrances which are not accessible shall have directional signage complying with 4.30.1, 4.30.2, 4.30.3, and 4.30.5, which indicates the location of the nearest accessible entrance.

(9)* In buildings or facilities, or portions of buildings or facilities, required to be accessible, accessible means of egress shall be provided in the same number as required for exits by local building/life safety regulations. Where a required exit from an occupiable level above or below a level of accessible exit discharge is not accessible, an area of rescue assistance shall be provided on each such level (in a number equal to that of inaccessible required exits). Areas of rescue assistance shall comply with 4.3.11. A horizontal exit, meeting the requirements of local building/life safety regulations, shall satisfy the requirement for an area of rescue assistance.

EXCEPTION: Areas of rescue assistance are not required in buildings or facilities having a supervised automatic sprinkler system.

(10)* Drinking Fountains:

(a) Where only one drinking fountain is provided on a floor there shall be a drinking fountain which is accessible to individuals who use wheelchairs in accordance with 4.15 and one accessible to those who have difficulty bending or stooping. (This can be accommodated by the use of a "hi-lo" fountain; by providing one fountain accessible to those who use wheelchairs and one fountain at a standard height convenient for those who have difficulty bending; by providing a fountain accessible under 4.15 and a water cooler; or by such other means as would achieve the required accessibility for each group on each floor.)

(b) Where more than one drinking fountain or water cooler is provided on a floor, 50% of those provided shall comply with 4.15 and shall be on an accessible route.

(11) Toilet Facilities: If toilet rooms are provided, then each public and common use toilet room shall comply with 4.22. Other toilet rooms provided for the use of occupants of specific spaces (i.e., a private toilet room for the occupant of a private office) shall be adaptable. If bathing rooms are provided, then each public and common use bathroom shall comply with 4.23. Accessible toilet rooms and bathing facilities shall be on an accessible route.

(12) Storage, Shelving and Display Units:

(a) If fixed or built-in storage facilities such as cabinets, shelves, closets, and drawers are provided in accessible spaces, at least one of each type provided shall contain storage space complying with 4.25. Additional storage may be provided outside of the dimensions required by 4.25.

(b) Shelves or display units allowing self-service by customers in mercantile occupancies shall be located on an accessible route complying with 4.3. Requirements for accessible reach range do not apply.

(13) Controls and operating mechanisms in accessible spaces, along accessible routes, or as parts of accessible elements (for

example, light switches and dispenser controls) shall comply with 4.27.

(14) If emergency warning systems are provided, then they shall include both audible alarms and visual alarms complying with 4.28. Sleeping accommodations required to comply with 9.3 shall have an alarm system complying with 4.28. Emergency warning systems in medical care facilities may be modified to suit standard health care alarm design practice.

Requirements for detectable warnings at curb ramps, hazardous vehicular areas, and reflecting pools have been suspended until July 26, 1998. By that date, the ATBCB should issue a joint final rule with the Departments of Justice and Transportation with respect to the need for and usability of current technical specifications for detectable warnings at curb ramps, hazardous vehicular areas, and reflecting pools.

(15) Detectable warnings shall be provided at locations as specified in 4.29.

(16) Building Signage:

(a) Signs which designate permanent rooms and spaces shall comply with 4.30.1, 4.30.4, 4.30.5 and 4.30.6.

(b) Other signs which provide direction to or information about functional spaces of the building shall comply with 4.30.1, 4.30.2, 4.30.3, and 4.30.5.

EXCEPTION: Building directories, menus, and all other signs which are temporary are not required to comply.

(17) Public telephones:

(a) If public pay telephones, public closed circuit telephones, or other public telephones are provided, then they shall comply with 4.31.2 through 4.31.8 to the extent required by the following table:

Number of each type of telephone provided on each floor	Number of telephones required to comply with 4.31.2 through 4.31.8[1]
1 or more single unit	1 per floor
1 bank[2]	1 per floor
2 or more banks[2]	1 per bank. Accessible unit may be installed as a single unit in proximity (either visible or with signage) to the bank. At least one public telephone per floor shall meet the requirements for a forward reach telephone [3].

[1] Additional public telephones may be installed at any height. Unless otherwise specified, accessible telephones may be either forward or side reach telephones.

[2] A bank consists of two or more adjacent public telephones, often installed as a unit.

[3] EXCEPTION: For exterior installations only, if dial tone first service is available, then a side reach telephone may be installed instead of the required forward reach telephone (i.e., one telephone in proximity to each bank shall comply with 4.31).

(b)* All telephones required to be accessible and complying with 4.31.2 through 4.31.8 shall be equipped with a volume control. In addition, 25 percent, but never less than one, of all other public telephones provided shall be equipped with a volume control and shall be dispersed among all types of public telephones, including closed circuit telephones, throughout the building or facility. Signage complying with applicable provisions of 4.30.7 shall be provided.

(c) The following shall be provided in accordance with 4.31.9:

(i) if a total number of four or more public pay telephones (including both interior and exterior phones) is provided at a site, and at least one is in an interior location, then at least one interior public text telephone shall be provided.

(ii) if an interior public pay telephone is provided in a stadium or arena, in a convention center, in a hotel with a convention center, or in a covered mall, at least one interior public text telephone shall be provided in the facility.

(iii) if a public pay telephone is located in or adjacent to a hospital emergency room, hospital recovery room, or hospital waiting room, one public text telephone shall be provided at each such location.

(d) Where a bank of telephones in the interior of a building consists of three or more public pay telephones, at least one public pay telephone in each such bank shall be equipped with a shelf and outlet in compliance with 4.31.9(2).

(18) If fixed or built-in seating or tables (including, but not limited to, study carrels and student laboratory stations), are provided in accessible public or common use areas, at least five percent (5%), but not less than one, of the fixed or built-in seating areas or tables shall comply with 4.32. An accessible route shall lead to and through such fixed or built-in seating areas, or tables.

(19)* Assembly areas:

(a) In places of assembly with fixed seating accessible wheelchair locations shall comply with 4.33.2, 4.33.3, and 4.33.4 and shall be provided consistent with the following table:

Capacity of Seating in Assembly Areas	Number of Required Wheelchair Locations
4 to 25	1
26 to 50	2
51 to 300	4
301 to 500	6
over 500	6, plus 1 additional space for each total seating capacity increase of 100

In addition, one percent, but not less than one, of all fixed seats shall be aisle seats with no armrests on the aisle side, or removable or folding armrests on the aisle side. Each such seat shall be identified by a sign or marker. Signage notifying patrons of the availability of such seats shall be posted at the ticket office. Aisle seats are not required to comply with 4.33.4.

(b) This paragraph applies to assembly areas where audible communications are integral to the use of the space (e.g., concert and lecture halls, playhouses and movie theaters, meeting rooms, etc.). Such assembly areas, if (1) they accommodate at least 50 persons, or if they have audio-amplification systems, and (2) they have fixed seating, shall have a permanently installed assistive listening system complying with 4.33. For other assembly areas, a permanently installed assistive listening system, or an adequate number of electrical outlets or other supplementary wiring necessary to support a portable assistive listening system shall be provided. The minimum number of receivers to be provided shall be equal to 4 percent of the total number of seats, but in no case less than two. Signage complying with applicable provisions of 4.30 shall be installed to notify patrons of the availability of a listening system.

(20) Where automated teller machines (ATMs) are provided, each ATM shall comply with the requirements of 4.34 except where two or more are provided at a location, then only one must comply.

EXCEPTION: Drive-up-only automated teller machines are not required to comply with 4.27.2, 4.27.3 and 4.34.3.

(21) Where dressing and fitting rooms are provided for use by the general public, patients, customers or employees, 5 percent, but never less than one, of dressing rooms for each type of use in each cluster of dressing rooms shall be accessible and shall comply with 4.35.

Examples of types of dressing rooms are those serving different genders or distinct and different functions as in different treatment or examination facilities.

4.1.4 (Reserved).

4.1.5 Accessible Buildings: Additions. Each addition to an existing building or facility shall be regarded as an alteration. Each space or element added to the existing building or facility shall comply with the applicable provisions of 4.1.1 to 4.1.3, Minimum Requirements (for New Construction) and the applicable technical specifications of 4.2 through 4.35 and sections 5 through 10. Each addition that affects or could affect the usability of an area containing a primary function shall comply with 4.1.6(2).

4.1.6 Accessible Buildings: Alterations.

(1) General. Alterations to existing buildings and facilities shall comply with the following:

(a) No alteration shall be undertaken which decreases or has the effect of decreasing accessibility or usability of a building or facility below the requirements for new construction at the time of alteration.

(b) If existing elements, spaces, or common areas are altered, then each such altered element, space, feature, or area shall comply with the applicable provisions of 4.1.1 to 4.1.3 Minimum Requirements (for New Construction). If the applicable provision for new construction requires that an element, space, or common area be on an accessible route, the altered element, space, or common area is not required to be on an accessible route except as provided in 4.1.6(2) (Alterations to an Area Containing a Primary Function.)

(c) If alterations of single elements, when considered together, amount to an alteration of a room or space in a building or facility, the entire space shall be made accessible.

(d) No alteration of an existing element, space, or area of a building or facility shall impose a requirement for greater accessibility than that which would be required for new construction. For example, if the elevators and stairs in a building are being altered and the elevators are, in turn, being made accessible, then no accessibility modifications are required to the stairs connecting levels connected by the elevator. If stair modifications to correct unsafe conditions are required by other codes, the modifications shall be done in compliance with these guidelines unless technically infeasible.

(e) At least one interior public text telephone complying with 4.31.9 shall be provided if:

(i) alterations to existing buildings or facilities with less than four exterior or interior public pay telephones would increase the total number to four or more telephones with at least one in an interior location; or

(ii) alterations to one or more exterior or interior public pay telephones occur in an existing building or facility with four or more public telephones with at least one in an interior location.

(f) If an escalator or stair is planned or installed where none existed previously and major structural modifications are necessary for such installation, then a means of accessible vertical access shall be provided that complies with the applicable provisions of 4.7, 4.8, 4.10, or 4.11.

(g) In alterations, the requirements of 4.1.3(9), 4.3.10 and 4.3.11 do not apply.

(h)* Entrances: If a planned alteration entails alterations to an entrance, and the building has an accessible entrance, the entrance being altered is not required to comply with 4.1.3(8), except to the extent required by 4.1.6(2). If a particular entrance is not made accessible, appropriate accessible signage indicating the location of the nearest accessible entrance(s) shall be installed at or near the inaccessible entrance, such that a person with disabilities will not be required to retrace the approach route from the inaccessible entrance.

(i) If the alteration work is limited solely to the electrical, mechanical, or plumbing system, or to hazardous material abatement, or automatic sprinkler retrofitting, and does not involve the alteration of any elements or spaces required to be accessible under these guidelines, then 4.1.6(2) does not apply.

(j) EXCEPTION: In alteration work, if compliance with 4.1.6 is technically infeasible, the alteration shall provide accessibility to the maximum extent feasible. Any elements or features of the building or facility that are being altered and can be made accessible shall be made accessible within the scope of the alteration.

Technically Infeasible. Means, with respect to an alteration of a building or a facility, that it has little likelihood of being accomplished because existing structural conditions would require removing or altering a load-bearing member which is an essential part of the structural frame; or because other existing physical or site constraints prohibit modification or addition of elements, spaces, or features which are in full and strict compliance with the minimum requirements for new construction and which are necessary to provide accessibility.

(k) EXCEPTION:

(i) These guidelines do not require the installation of an elevator in an altered facility that is less than three stories or has less than 3,000 square feet per story unless the building is a shopping center, a shopping mall, the professional office of a health care provider, or another type of facility as determined by the Attorney General.

(ii) The exemption provided in paragraph (i) does not obviate or limit in any way the obligation to comply with the other accessibility requirements established in these guidelines. For example, alterations to floors above or below the ground floor must be accessible regardless of whether the altered facility has an elevator. If a facility subject to the elevator exemption set forth in paragraph (i) nonetheless has a full passenger elevator, that elevator shall meet, to the maximum extent feasible, the accessibility requirements of these guidelines.

(2) Alterations to an Area Containing a Primary Function: In addition to the requirements of 4.1.6(1), an alteration that affects or could affect the usability of or access to an area containing a primary function shall be made so as to ensure that, to the maximum extent feasible, the path of travel to the altered area and the restrooms, telephones, and drinking fountains serving the altered area, are readily accessible to and usable by individuals with disabilities, unless such alterations are disproportionate to the overall alterations in terms of cost and scope (as determined under criteria established by the Attorney General).

(3) Special Technical Provisions for Alterations to Existing Buildings and Facilities:

(a) Ramps: Curb ramps and interior or exterior ramps to be constructed on sites or in existing buildings or facilities where space limitations prohibit the use of a 1:12 slope or less may have slopes and rises as follows:
(i) A slope between 1:10 and 1:12 is allowed for a maximum rise of 6 inches.

(ii) A slope between 1:8 and 1:10 is allowed for a maximum rise of 3 inches. A slope steeper than 1:8 is not allowed.

(b) Stairs: Full extension of handrails at stairs shall not be required in alterations where such extensions would be hazardous or impossible due to plan configuration.

(c) Elevators:

(i) If safety door edges are provided in existing automatic elevators, automatic door reopening devices may be omitted (see 4.10.6).

(ii) Where existing shaft configuration or technical infeasibility prohibits strict compliance with 4.10.9, the minimum car plan dimensions may be reduced by the minimum amount necessary, but in no case shall the inside car area be smaller than 48 in by 48 in.

(iii) Equivalent facilitation may be provided with an elevator car of different dimensions when usability can be demonstrated and when all other elements required to be accessible comply with the applicable provisions of 4.10. For example, an elevator of 47 in by 69 in (1195 mm by 1755 mm) with a door opening on the narrow dimension, could accommodate the standard wheelchair clearances shown in Figure 4.

(d) Doors:

(i) Where it is technically infeasible to comply with clear opening width requirements of 4.13.5, a projection of 5/8 in maximum will be permitted for the latch side stop.

(ii) If existing thresholds are 3/4 in high or less, and have (or are modified to have) a beveled edge on each side, they may remain.

(e) Toilet Rooms:

(i) Where it is technically infeasible to comply with 4.22 or 4.23, the installation of at least one unisex toilet/bathroom per floor, located in the same area as existing toilet facilities, will be permitted in lieu of modifying existing toilet facilities to be accessible. Each unisex toilet room shall contain one water closet complying with 4.16 and one lavatory complying with 4.19, and the door shall have a privacy latch.
(ii) Where it is technically infeasible to install a required standard stall (Fig. 30(a)), or where other codes prohibit reduction of the fixture count (i.e., removal of a water closet in order to create a double-wide stall), either alternate stall (Fig.30(b)) may be provided in lieu of the standard stall.

(iii) When existing toilet or bathing facilities are being altered and are not made accessible, signage complying with 4.30.1, 4.30.2, 4.30.3, 4.30.5, and 4.30.7 shall be provided indicating the location of the nearest accessible toilet or bathing facility within the facility.
(f) Assembly Areas:

(i) Where it is technically infeasible to disperse accessible seating throughout an altered assembly area, accessible seating areas may be clustered. Each accessible seating area shall have provisions for companion seating and shall be located on an accessible route that also serves as a means of emergency egress.

(ii) Where it is technically infeasible to alter all performing areas to be on an accessible route, at least one of each type of performing area shall be made accessible.

(g) Platform Lifts (Wheelchair Lifts): In alterations, platform lifts (wheelchair lifts) complying with 4.11 and applicable state or local codes may be used as part of an accessible route. The use of lifts is not limited to the four conditions in exception 4 of 4.1.3(5)

(h) Dressing Rooms: In alterations where technical infeasibility can be demonstrated, one dressing room for each sex on each level shall be made accessible. Where only unisex dressing rooms are provided, accessible unisex dressing rooms may be used to fulfill this requirement.

4.1.7 Accessible Buildings: Historic Preservation.

(1) Applicability:

(a) General Rule. Alterations to a qualified historic building or facility shall comply with 4.1.6 Accessible Buildings: Alterations, the applicable technical specifications of 4.2 through 4.35 and the applicable special application sections 5 through 10 unless it is determined in accordance with the procedures in 4.1.7(2) that compliance with the requirements for accessible routes (exterior and interior), ramps, entrances, or toilets would threaten or destroy the historic significance of the building or facility in which case the alternative requirements in 4.1.7(3) may be used for the feature.

EXCEPTION: (Reserved).

(b) Definition. A qualified historic building or facility is a building or facility that is:

(i) Listed in or eligible for listing in the National Register of Historic Places; or

(ii) Designated as historic under an appropriate State or local law.

(2) Procedures:

(a) Alterations to Qualified Historic Buildings and Facilities Subject to Section 106 of the National Historic Preservation Act:

(i) Section 106 Process. Section 106 of the National Historic Preservation Act (16 U.S.C. 470 f) requires that a Federal agency with jurisdiction over a Federal, federally assisted, or federally licensed undertaking consider the effects of the agency's undertaking on buildings and facilities listed in or eligible for listing in the National Register of Historic Places and give the Advisory Council on Historic Preservation a reasonable opportunity to comment on the undertaking prior to approval of the undertaking.

(ii) ADA Application. Where alterations are undertaken to a qualified historic building or facility that is subject to section 106 of the National Historic Preservation Act, the Federal agency with jurisdiction over the undertaking shall follow the section 106 process. If the State Historic Preservation Officer or Advisory Council on Historic Preservation agrees that compliance with the requirements for accessible routes (exterior and interior), ramps, entrances, or toilets would threaten or destroy the historic significance of the building or facility, the alternative requirements in 4.1.7(3) may be used for the feature.

(b) Alterations to Qualified Historic Buildings and Facilities Not Subject to Section 106 of the National Historic Preservation Act. Where alterations are undertaken to a qualified historic building or facility that is not subject to section 106 of the National Historic Preservation Act, if the entity undertaking the alterations believes that compliance with the requirements for accessible routes (exterior and interior), ramps, entrances, or toilets would threaten or destroy the historic significance of the building or facility and that the alternative requirements in 4.1.7(3) should be used for the feature, the entity should consult with the State Historic Preservation Officer. If the State Historic Preservation Officer agrees that compliance with the accessibility requirements for accessible routes (exterior and interior), ramps, entrances or toilets would threaten or destroy the historical significance of the building or facility, the alternative requirements in 4.1.7(3) may be used.

(c) Consultation With Interested Persons. Interested persons should be invited to participate in the consultation process, including State or local accessibility officials, individuals with disabilities, and organizations representing individuals with disabilities.

(d) Certified Local Government Historic Preservation Programs. Where the State Historic Preservation Officer has delegated the consultation responsibility for purposes of this section to a local government historic preservation program that has been certified in accordance with section 101(c) of the National Historic Preservation Act of 1966 (16 U.S.C. 470a (c)) and implementing regulations (36 CFR 61.5), the responsibility may be carried out by the appropriate local government body or official.

(3) Historic Preservation: Minimum Requirements:

(a) At least one accessible route complying with 4.3 from a site access point to an accessible entrance shall be provided.

EXCEPTION: A ramp with a slope no greater than 1:6 for a run not to exceed 2 ft (610 mm) may be used as part of an accessible route to an entrance.

(b) At least one accessible entrance complying with 4.14 which is used by the public shall be provided.
EXCEPTION: If it is determined that no entrance used by the public can comply with 4.14, then access at any entrance not used by the general public but open (unlocked) with directional signage at the primary entrance may be used. The accessible entrance shall also have a notification system. Where security is a problem, remote monitoring may be used.

(c) If toilets are provided, then at least one toilet facility complying with 4.22 and 4.1.6 shall be provided along an accessible route that complies with 4.3. Such toilet facility may be unisex in design.

(d) Accessible routes from an accessible entrance to all publicly used spaces on at least the level of the accessible entrance shall be provided. Access shall be provided to all levels of a building or facility in compliance with 4.1 whenever practical.

(e) Displays and written information, documents, etc., should be located where they can be seen by a seated person. Exhibits and signage displayed horizontally (e.g., open books), should be no higher than 44 in (1120 mm) above the floor surface.

NOTE: The technical provisions of sections 4.2 through 4.35 are the same as those of the American National Standard Institute's document A117.1-1980, except as noted in the text.

4.2 Space Allowance and Reach Ranges.

4.2.1* Wheelchair Passage Width. The minimum clear width for single wheelchair passage shall be 32 in (815 mm) at a point and 36 in (915 mm) continuously (see Fig. 1 and 24(e)).

4.2.2 Width for Wheelchair Passing. The minimum width for two wheelchairs to pass is 60 in (1525 mm) (see Fig. 2).

4.2.3* Wheelchair Turning Space. The space required for a wheelchair to make a 180-degree turn is a clear space of 60 in (1525 mm) diameter (see Fig. 3(a)) or a T-shaped space (see Fig. 3(b)).

4.2.4* Clear Floor or Ground Space for Wheelchairs.

4.2.4.1 Size and Approach. The minimum clear floor or ground space required to accommodate a single, stationary wheelchair and occupant is 30 in by 48 in (760 mm by 1220 mm) (see Fig. 4(a)). The minimum clear floor or ground space for wheelchairs may be positioned for forward or parallel approach to an object (see Fig 4(b) and (c)). Clear floor or ground space for wheelchairs may be part of the knee space required under some objects.

4.2.4.2 Relationship of Maneuvering Clearance to Wheelchair Spaces. One full unobstructed side of the clear floor or ground space for a wheelchair shall adjoin or overlap an accessible route or adjoin another wheelchair clear floor space. If a clear floor space is located in an alcove or otherwise confined on all or part of three sides, additional maneuvering clearances shall be provided as shown in Fig. 4(d) and (e).

4.2.4.3 Surfaces for Wheelchair Spaces. Clear floor or ground spaces for wheelchairs shall comply with 4.5.

4.2.5* Forward Reach. If the clear floor space only allows forward approach to an object, the maximum high forward reach allowed shall be 48 in (1220 mm) (see Fig. 5(a)). The minimum low forward reach is 15 in (380 mm). If the high forward reach is over an obstruction, reach and clearances shall be as shown in

Fig. 5(b).

4.2.6* Side Reach. If the clear floor space allows parallel approach by a person in a wheelchair, the maximum high side reach allowed shall be 54 in (1370 mm) and the low side reach shall be no less than 9 in (230 mm) above the floor (Fig. 6(a) and (b)). If the side reach is over an obstruction, the reach and clearances shall be as shown in Fig 6(c).

4.3 Accessible Route.

4.3.1* General. All walks, halls, corridors, aisles, skywalks, tunnels, and other spaces that are part of an accessible route shall comply with 4.3.

4.3.2 Location.

(1) At least one accessible route within the boundary of the site shall be provided from public transportation stops, accessible parking, and accessible passenger loading zones, and public streets or sidewalks to the accessible building entrance they serve. The accessible route shall, to the maximum extent feasible, coincide with the route for the general public.

(2) At least one accessible route shall connect accessible buildings, facilities, elements, and spaces that are on the same site.

(3) At least one accessible route shall connect accessible building or facility entrances with all accessible spaces and elements and with all accessible dwelling units within the building or facility.

(4) An accessible route shall connect at least one accessible entrance of each accessible dwelling unit with those exterior and interior spaces and facilities that serve the accessible dwelling unit.

4.3.3 Width. The minimum clear width of an accessible route shall be 36 in (915 mm) except at doors (see 4.13.5 and 4.13.6). If a person in a wheelchair must make a turn around an obstruction, the minimum clear width of the accessible route shall be as shown in Fig. 7(a) and (b).

4.3.4 Passing Space. If an accessible route has less than 60 in (1525 mm) clear width, then passing spaces at least 60 in by 60 in (1525 mm by 1525 mm) shall be located at reasonable intervals not to exceed 200 ft (61 m). A T-intersection of two corridors or walks is an acceptable passing place.

4.3.5 Head Room. Accessible routes shall comply with 4.4.2.

4.3.6 Surface Textures. The surface of an accessible route shall comply with 4.5.

4.3.7 Slope. An accessible route with a running slope greater than 1:20 is a ramp and shall comply with 4.8. Nowhere shall the cross slope of an accessible route exceed 1:50.

4.3.8 Changes in Levels. Changes in levels along an accessible route shall comply with 4.5.2. If an accessible route has changes in level greater than 1/2 in (13 mm), then a curb ramp, ramp, elevator, or platform lift (as permitted in 4.1.3 and 4.1.6) shall be provided that complies with 4.7, 4.8, 4.10, or 4.11, respectively. An accessible route does not include stairs, steps, or escalators. See definition of "egress, means of" in 3.5.

4.3.9 Doors. Doors along an accessible route shall comply with 4.13.

4.3.10* Egress. Accessible routes serving any accessible space or element shall also serve as a means of egress for emergencies or connect to an accessible area of rescue assistance.

4.3.11 Areas of Rescue Assistance.

4.3.11.1 Location and Construction. An area of rescue assistance shall be one of the following:
(1) A portion of a stairway landing within a smokeproof enclosure (complying with local requirements).

(2) A portion of an exterior exit balcony located immediately adjacent to an exit stairway when the balcony complies with local requirements for exterior exit balconies. Openings to the interior of the building located within 20 feet (6 m) of the area of rescue assistance shall be protected with fire assemblies having a three-fourths hour fire protection rating.

(3) A portion of a one-hour fire-resistive corridor (complying with local requirements for fire-resistive construction and for openings) located immediately adjacent to an exit enclosure.

(4) A vestibule located immediately adjacent to an exit enclosure and constructed to the same fire-resistive standards as required for corridors and openings.

(5) A portion of a stairway landing within an exit enclosure which is vented to the exterior and is separated from the interior of the building with not less than one-hour fire-resistive doors.

(6) When approved by the appropriate local authority, an area or a room which is separated from other portions of the building by a smoke barrier. Smoke barriers shall have a fire-resistive rating of not less than one hour and shall completely enclose the area or room. Doors in the smoke barrier shall be tight-fitting smoke- and draft-control assemblies having a fire-protection rating of not less than 20 minutes and shall be self-closing or automatic closing. The area or room shall be provided with an exit directly to an exit enclosure. Where the room or area exits into an exit enclosure which is required to be of more than one-hour fire- resistive construction, the room or area shall have the same fire- resistive construction, including the same opening protection, as required for the adjacent exit enclosure.

(7) An elevator lobby when elevator shafts and adjacent lobbies are pressurized as required for smokeproof enclosures by local regulations and when complying with requirements herein for size, communication, and signage. Such pressurization system shall be activated by smoke detectors on each floor located in a manner approved by the appropriate local authority.

Pressurization equipment and its duct work within the building shall be separated from other portions of the building by a minimum two-hour fire- resistive construction.

4.3.11.2 Size. Each area of rescue assistance shall provide at least two accessible areas each being not less than 30 inches by 48 inches (760 mm by 1220 mm). The area of rescue assistance shall not encroach on any required exit width. The total number of such 30-inch by 48-inch (760 mm by 1220 mm) areas per story shall be not less than one for every 200 persons of calculated occupant load served by the area of rescue assistance.

EXCEPTION: The appropriate local authority may reduce the minimum number of 30-inch by 48-inch (760 mm by 1220 mm) areas to one for each area of rescue assistance on floors where the occupant load is less than 200.

4.3.11.3* Stairway Width. Each stairway adjacent to an area of rescue assistance shall have a minimum clear width of 48 inches between handrails.

4.3.11.4* Two-way Communication. A method of two-way communication, with both visible and audible signals, shall be provided between each area of rescue assistance and the primary entry. The fire department or appropriate local authority may approve a location other than the primary entry.

4.3.11.5 Identification. Each area of rescue assistance shall be identified by a sign which states "AREA OF RESCUE ASSISTANCE" and displays the international symbol of accessibility. The sign shall be illuminated when exit sign illumination is required. Signage shall also be installed at all inaccessible exits and where otherwise necessary to clearly indicate the direction to areas of rescue assistance. In each area of rescue assistance, instructions on the use of the area under emergency conditions shall be posted adjoining the two-way communication system.

4.4 Protruding Objects.

4.4.1* General. Objects projecting from walls (for example, telephones) with their leading edges between 27 in and 80 in (685 mm and 2030 mm) above the finished floor shall protrude no more than 4 in (100 mm) into walks, halls, corridors, passageways, or isles (see Fig. 8(a)). Objects mounted with their leading edges at or below 27 in (685 mm) above the finished floor may protrude any amount (see Fig. 8(a) and (b)). Free-standing objects mounted on posts or pylons may overhang 12 in (305 mm) maximum from 27 in to 80 in (685 mm to 2030 mm) above the ground or finished floor (see Fig. 8(c) and (d)). Protruding objects shall not reduce the clear width of an accessible route or maneuvering space (see Fig. 8(e)).

4.4.2 Head Room. Walks, halls, corridors, passageways, aisles, or other circulation spaces shall have 80 in (2030 mm) minimum clear head room (see Fig. 8(a)). If vertical clearance of an area adjoining an accessible route is reduced to less than 80 in (nominal dimension), a barrier to warn blind or visually-impaired persons shall be provided (see Fig. 8(c-1)).

4.5 Ground and Floor Surfaces.

4.5.1* General. Ground and floor surfaces along accessible routes and in accessible rooms and spaces including floors, walks, ramps, stairs, and curb ramps, shall be stable, firm, slip-resistant, and shall comply with 4.5.

4.5.2 Changes in Level. Changes in level up to 1/4 in (6 mm) may be vertical and without edge treatment (see Fig. 7(c)). Changes in level between 1/4 in and 1/2 in (6 mm and 13 mm) shall be beveled with a slope no greater than 1:2 (see Fig. 7(d)). Changes in level greater than 1/2 in (13 mm) shall be accomplished by means of a ramp that complies with 4.7 or 4.8.

4.5.3* Carpet. If carpet or carpet tile is used on a ground or floor surface, then it shall be securely attached; have a firm cushion, pad, or backing, or no cushion or pad; and have a level loop, textured loop, level cut pile, or level cut/uncut pile texture. The maximum pile thickness shall be 1/2 in (13 mm) (see Fig. 8(f)). Exposed edges of carpet shall be fastened to floor surfaces and have trim along the entire length of the exposed edge. Carpet edge trim shall comply with 4.5.2.

4.5.4 Gratings. If gratings are located in walking surfaces, then they shall have spaces no greater than 1/2 in (13 mm) wide in one direction (see Fig. 8(g)). If gratings have elongated openings, then they shall be placed so that the long dimension is perpendicular to the dominant direction of travel (see Fig. 8(h)).

4.6 Parking and Passenger Loading Zones.

4.6.1 Minimum Number. Parking spaces required to be accessible by 4.1 shall comply with 4.6.2 through 4.6.5. Passenger loading zones required to be accessible by 4.1 shall comply with 4.6.5 and 4.6.6.

4.6.2 Location. Accessible parking spaces serving a particular building shall be located on the shortest accessible route of travel from adjacent parking to an accessible entrance. In parking facilities that do not serve a particular building, accessible parking shall be located on the shortest accessible route of travel to an accessible pedestrian entrance of the parking facility. In buildings with multiple accessible entrances with adjacent parking, accessible parking spaces shall be dispersed and located closest to the accessible entrances.

4.6.3* Parking Spaces. Accessible parking spaces shall be at least 96 in (2440 mm) wide. Parking access aisles shall be part of an accessible route to the building or facility entrance and shall comply with 4.3. Two accessible parking spaces may share a common access aisle (see Fig. 9). Parked vehicle overhangs shall not reduce the clear width of an accessible route. Parking spaces and access aisles shall be level with surface slopes not exceeding 1:50 (2%) in all directions.

4.6.4* Signage. Accessible parking spaces shall be designated as reserved by a sign showing the symbol of accessibility (see 4.30.7). Spaces complying with 4.1.2(5)(b) shall have an additional sign "Van-Accessible" mounted below the symbol of accessibility. Such signs shall be located so they cannot be obscured by a vehicle parked in the space.

4.6.5* Vertical Clearance. Provide minimum vertical clearance of 114 in (2895 mm) at accessible passenger loading zones and along at least one vehicle access route to such areas from site entrance(s) and exit(s). At parking spaces complying with 4.1.2(5)(b), provide minimum vertical clearance of 98 in (2490 mm) at the parking space and along at least one vehicle access route to such spaces from site entrance(s) and exit(s).

4.6.6 Passenger Loading Zones. Passenger loading zones shall provide an access aisle at least 60 in (1525 mm) wide and 20 ft (240 in) (6100 mm) long adjacent and parallel to the vehicle pull-up space (see Fig. 10). If there are curbs between the access aisle and the vehicle pull-up space, then a curb ramp complying with 4.7 shall be provided. Vehicle standing spaces and access aisles shall be level with surface slopes not exceeding 1:50 (2%) in all directions.

4.7 Curb Ramps.

4.7.1 Location. Curb ramps complying with 4.7 shall be provided wherever an accessible route crosses a curb.

4.7.2 Slope. Slopes of curb ramps shall comply with 4.8.2. The slope shall be measured as shown in Fig. 11. Transitions from ramps to walks, gutters, or streets shall be flush and free of abrupt changes. Maximum slopes of adjoining gutters, road surface immediately adjacent to the curb ramp, or accessible route shall not exceed 1:20.

4.7.3 Width. The minimum width of a curb ramp shall be 36 in (915 mm), exclusive of flared sides.

4.7.4 Surface. Surfaces of curb ramps shall comply with 4.5.

4.7.5 Sides of Curb Ramps. If a curb ramp is located where pedestrians must walk across the ramp, or where it is not protected by handrails or guardrails, it shall have flared sides; the maximum slope of the flare shall be 1:10 (see Fig. 12(a)). Curb ramps with returned curbs may be used where pedestrians would not normally walk across the ramp (see Fig. 12(b)).

4.7.6 Built-up Curb Ramps. Built-up curb ramps shall be located so that they do not project into vehicular traffic lanes (see Fig. 13).

Requirements for detectable warnings at curb ramps, hazardous vehicular areas, and reflecting pools have been suspended until July 26, 1998. By that date, the ATBCB should issue a joint final rule with the Departments of Justice and Transportation with respect to the need for and usability of current technical specifications for detectable warnings at curb ramps, hazardous vehicular areas, and reflecting pools.

4.7.7 Detectable Warnings. [Provision suspended until July 26, 1998] A curb ramp shall have a detectable warning complying with 4.29.2. The detectable warning shall extend the full width and depth of the curb ramp.

4.7.8 Obstructions. Curb ramps shall be located or protected to prevent their obstruction by parked vehicles.

4.7.9 Location at Marked Crossings. Curb ramps at marked crossings shall be wholly contained within the markings, excluding any flared sides (see Fig. 15).

4.7.10 Diagonal Curb Ramps. If diagonal (or corner type) curb ramps have returned curbs or other well-defined edges, such edges shall be parallel to the direction of pedestrian flow. The bottom of diagonal curb ramps shall have 48 in (1220 mm) minimum clear space as shown in Fig. 15(c) and (d). If diagonal curb ramps are provided at marked crossings, the 48 in (1220 mm) clear space shall be within the markings (see Fig. 15(c) and (d)). If diagonal curb ramps have flared sides, they shall also have at least a 24 in (610 mm) long segment of straight curb located on each side of the curb ramp and within the marked crossing (see Fig. 15(c)).

4.7.11 Islands. Any raised islands in crossings shall be cut through level with the street or have curb ramps at both sides and a level area at least 48 in (1220 mm) long between the curb ramps in the part of the island intersected by the crossings (see Fig. 15(a) and (b)).

4.8 Ramps.

4.8.1* General. Any part of an accessible route with a slope greater than 1:20 shall be considered a ramp and shall comply with 4.8.

4.8.2* Slope and Rise. The least possible slope shall be used for any ramp. The maximum slope of a ramp in new construction shall be 1:12. The maximum rise for any run shall be 30 in (760 mm) (see Fig. 16). Curb ramps and ramps to be constructed on existing sites or in existing buildings or facilities may have slopes and rises as allowed in 4.1.6(3)(a) if space limitations prohibit the use of a 1:12 slope or less.

4.8.3 Clear Width. The minimum clear width of a ramp shall be 36 in (915 mm).

4.8.4* Landings. Ramps shall have level landings at bottom and top of each ramp and each ramp run. Landings shall have the following features:

(1) The landing shall be at least as wide as the ramp run leading to it.

(2) The landing length shall be a minimum of 60 in (1525 mm) clear.

(3) If ramps change direction at landings, the minimum landing size shall be 60 in by 60 in (1525 mm by 1525 mm).

(4) If a doorway is located at a landing, then the area in front of the doorway shall comply with 4.13.6.

4.8.5* Handrails. If a ramp run has a rise greater than 6 in (150 mm) or a horizontal projection greater than 72 in (1830 mm), then it shall have handrails on both sides. Handrails are not required on curb ramps or adjacent to seating in assembly areas. Handrails shall comply with 4.26 and shall have the following features:

(1) Handrails shall be provided along both sides of ramp segments. The inside handrail on switchback or dogleg ramps shall always be continuous.

(2) If handrails are not continuous, they shall extend at least 12 in (305 mm) beyond the top and bottom of the ramp segment and shall be parallel with the floor or ground surface (see Fig. 17).

(3) The clear space between the handrail and the wall shall be 1-1/2 in (38 mm).

(4) Gripping surfaces shall be continuous.

(5) Top of handrail gripping surfaces shall be mounted between 34 in and 38 in (865 mm and 965 mm) above ramp surfaces.

(6) Ends of handrails shall be either rounded or returned smoothly to floor, wall, or post.

(7) Handrails shall not rotate within their fittings.

4.8.6 Cross Slope and Surfaces. The cross slope of ramp surfaces shall be no greater than 1:50. Ramp surfaces shall comply with 4.5.

4.8.7 Edge Protection. Ramps and landings with drop-offs shall have curbs, walls, railings, or projecting surfaces that prevent people from slipping off the ramp. Curbs shall be a minimum of 2 in (50 mm) high (see Fig. 17).

4.8.8 Outdoor Conditions. Outdoor ramps and their approaches shall be designed so that water will not accumulate on walking surfaces.

4.9 Stairs.

4.9.1* Minimum Number. Stairs required to be accessible by 4.1 shall comply with 4.9.

4.9.2 Treads and Risers. On any given flight of stairs, all steps shall have uniform riser heights and uniform tread widths. Stair treads shall be no less than 11 in (280 mm) wide, measured from riser to riser (see Fig. 18(a)). Open risers are not permitted.

4.9.3 Nosings. The undersides of nosings shall not be abrupt. The radius of curvature at the leading edge of the tread shall be no greater than 1/2 in (13 mm). Risers shall be sloped or the underside of the nosing shall have an angle not less than 60 degrees from the horizontal. Nosings shall project no more than 1-1/2 in (38 mm) (see Fig. 18).

4.9.4 Handrails. Stairways shall have handrails at both sides of all stairs. Handrails shall comply with 4.26 and shall have the following features:

(1) Handrails shall be continuous along both sides of stairs. The inside handrail on switchback or dogleg stairs shall always be continuous (see Fig. 19(a) and (b)).
(2) If handrails are not continuous, they shall extend at least 12 in (305 mm) beyond the top riser and at least 12 in (305 mm) plus the width of one tread beyond the bottom riser. At the top, the extension shall be parallel with the floor or ground surface.

At the bottom, the handrail shall continue to slope for a distance of the width of one tread from the bottom riser; the remainder of the extension shall be horizontal (see Fig. 19(c) and (d)). Handrail extensions shall comply with 4.4.

(3) The clear space between handrails and wall shall be 1-1/2 in (38 mm).

(4) Gripping surfaces shall be uninterrupted by newel posts, other construction elements, or obstructions.

(5) Top of handrail gripping surface shall be mounted between 34 in and 38 in (865 mm and 965 mm) above stair nosings.

(6) Ends of handrails shall be either rounded or returned smoothly to floor, wall or post.

(7) Handrails shall not rotate within their fittings.

4.9.5 Detectable Warnings at Stairs. (Reserved).

4.9.6 Outdoor Conditions. Outdoor stairs and their approaches shall be designed so that water will not accumulate on walking surfaces.

4.10 Elevators.

4.10.1 General. Accessible elevators shall be on an accessible route and shall comply with 4.10 and with the ASME A17.1-1990, Safety Code for Elevators and Escalators. Freight elevators shall not be considered as meeting the requirements of this section unless the only elevators provided are used as combination passenger and freight elevators for the public and employees.

4.10.2 Automatic Operation. Elevator operation shall be automatic. Each car shall be equipped with a self-leveling feature that will automatically bring the car to floor landings within a tolerance of 1/2 in (13 mm) under rated loading to zero loading conditions. This self-leveling feature shall be automatic and independent of the operating device and shall correct the overtravel or undertravel.

4.10.3 Hall Call Buttons. Call buttons in elevator lobbies and halls shall be centered at 42 in (1065 mm) above the floor. Such call buttons shall have visual signals to indicate when each call is registered and when each call is answered. Call buttons shall be a minimum of 3/4 in (19 mm) in the smallest dimension. The button designating the up direction shall be on top. (See Fig. 20.) Buttons shall be raised or flush. Objects mounted beneath hall call buttons shall not project into the elevator lobby more than 4 in (100 mm).

4.10.4 Hall Lanterns. A visible and audible signal shall be provided at each hoistway entrance to indicate which car is answering a call. Audible signals shall sound once for the up direction and twice for the down direction or shall have verbal annunciators that say "up" or "down." Visible signals shall have the following features:

(1) Hall lantern fixtures shall be mounted so that their centerline is at least 72 in (1830 mm) above the lobby floor. (See Fig. 20.)

(2) Visual elements shall be at least 2-1/2 in (64 mm) in the smallest dimension.

(3) Signals shall be visible from the vicinity of the hall call button (see Fig. 20). In-car lanterns located in cars, visible from the vicinity of hall call buttons, and conforming to the above requirements, shall be acceptable.

4.10.5 Raised and Braille Characters on Hoistway Entrances. All elevator hoistway entrances shall have raised and Braille floor designations provided on both jambs. The centerline of the characters shall be 60 in (1525 mm) above finish floor. Such characters shall be 2 in (50 mm) high and shall comply with 4.30.4. Permanently applied plates are acceptable if they are permanently fixed to the jambs. (See Fig. 20).

4.10.6* Door Protective and Reopening Device. Elevator doors shall open and close automatically. They shall be provided with a reopening device that will stop and reopen a car door and hoistway door automatically if the door becomes obstructed by an object or person. The device shall be capable of completing these operations without requiring contact for an obstruction passing through the opening at heights of 5 in and 29 in (125 mm and 735 mm) above finish floor (see Fig. 20). Door reopening devices shall remain effective for at least 20 seconds. After such an interval, doors may close in accordance with the requirements of ASME A17.1-1990.

4.10.7* Door and Signal Timing for Hall Calls. The minimum acceptable time from notification that a car is answering a call until the doors of that car start to close shall be calculated from the following equation:

$$T = D/(1.5 \text{ ft/s}) \text{ or } T = D/(445 \text{ mm/s})$$

where T total time in seconds and D distance (in feet or millimeters) from a point in the lobby or corridor 60 in (1525 mm) directly in front of the farthest call button controlling that car to the centerline of its hoistway door (see Fig. 21). For cars with in-car lanterns, T begins when the lantern is visible from the vicinity of hall call buttons and an audible signal is sounded. The minimum acceptable notification time shall be 5 seconds.

4.10.8 Door Delay for Car Calls. The minimum time for elevator doors to remain fully open in response to a car call shall be 3 seconds.

4.10.9 Floor Plan of Elevator Cars. The floor area of elevator cars shall provide space for wheelchair users to enter the car, maneuver within reach of controls, and exit from the car. Acceptable door opening and inside dimensions shall be as shown in Fig. 22. The clearance between the car platform sill and the edge of any hoistway landing shall be no greater than 1-1/4 in (32 mm).

4.10.10 Floor Surfaces. Floor surfaces shall comply with 4.5.

4.10.11 Illumination Levels. The level of illumination at the car controls, platform, and car threshold and landing sill shall be at least 5 footcandles (53.8 lux).

4.10.12* Car Controls. Elevator control panels shall have the following features:

(1) Buttons. All control buttons shall be at least 3/4 in (19 mm) in their smallest dimension. They shall be raised or flush.

(2) Tactile, Braille, and Visual Control Indicators. All control buttons shall be designated by Braille and by raised standard alphabet characters for letters, arabic characters for numerals, or standard symbols as shown in Fig. 23(a), and as required in ASME A17.1-1990. Raised and Braille characters and symbols shall comply with 4.30. The call button for the main entry floor shall be designated by a raised star at the left of the floor designation (see Fig. 23(a)). All raised designations for control buttons shall be placed immediately to the left of the button to which they apply. Applied plates, permanently attached, are an acceptable means to provide raised control designations. Floor buttons shall be provided with visual indicators to show when each call is registered. The visual indicators shall be extinguished when each call is answered.

(3) Height. All floor buttons shall be no higher than 54 in (1370 mm) above the finish floor for side approach and 48 in (1220 mm) for front approach. Emergency controls, including the emergency alarm and emergency stop, shall be grouped at the bottom of the panel and shall have their centerlines no less than 35 in (890 mm) above the finish floor (see Fig. 23(a) and (b)).

(4) Location. Controls shall be located on a front wall if cars have center opening doors, and at the side wall or at the front wall next to the door if cars have side opening doors (see Fig. 23(c) and (d)).

4.10.13* Car Position Indicators. In elevator cars, a visual car position indicator shall be provided above the car control panel or over the door to show the position of the elevator in the hoistway. As the car passes or stops at a floor served by the elevators, the corresponding numerals shall illuminate, and an audible signal shall sound. Numerals shall be a minimum of 1/2 in (13 mm) high. The audible signal shall be no less than 20 decibels with a frequency no higher than 1500 Hz. An automatic verbal announcement of the floor number at which a car stops or which a car passes may be substituted for the audible signal.

4.10.14* Emergency Communications. If provided, emergency two-way communication systems between the elevator and a point outside the hoistway shall comply with ASME A17.1-1990. The highest operable part of a two-way communication system shall be a maximum of 48 in (1220 mm) from the floor of the car. It shall be identified by a raised symbol and lettering complying with 4.30 and located adjacent to the device. If the system uses a handset then the length of the cord from the panel to the handset shall be at least 29 in (735 mm). If the system is located in a closed compartment the compartment door hardware shall conform to 4.27, Controls and Operating Mechanisms. The emergency intercommunication system shall not require voice communication.

4.11 Platform Lifts (Wheelchair Lifts).

4.11.1 Location. Platform lifts (wheelchair lifts) permitted by 4.1 shall comply with the requirements of 4.11.

4.11.2* Other Requirements. If platform lifts (wheelchair lifts) are used, they shall comply with 4.2.4, 4.5, 4.27, and ASME A17.1 Safety Code for Elevators and Escalators, Section XX, 1990.

4.11.3 Entrance. If platform lifts are used then they shall facilitate unassisted entry, operation, and exit from the lift in compliance with 4.11.2.

4.12 Windows.

4.12.1* General. (Reserved).

4.12.2* Window Hardware. (Reserved).

4.13 Doors.

4.13.1 General. Doors required to be accessible by 4.1 shall comply with the requirements of 4.13.

4.13.2 Revolving Doors and Turnstiles. Revolving doors or turnstiles shall not be the only means of passage at an accessible entrance or along an accessible route. An accessible gate or door shall be provided adjacent to the turnstile or revolving door and shall be so designed as to facilitate the same use pattern.

4.13.3 Gates. Gates, including ticket gates, shall meet all applicable specifications of 4.13.

4.13.4 Double-Leaf Doorways. If doorways have two independently operated door leaves, then at least one leaf shall meet the specifications in 4.13.5 and 4.13.6. That leaf shall be an active leaf.

4.13.5 Clear Width. Doorways shall have a minimum clear opening of 32 in (815 mm) with the door open 90 degrees, measured between the face of the door and the opposite stop (see Fig. 24(a), (b), (c), and (d)). Openings more than 24 in (610 mm) in depth shall comply with 4.2.1 and 4.3.3 (see Fig. 24(e)).

EXCEPTION: Doors not requiring full user passage, such as shallow closets, may have the clear opening reduced to 20 in (510 mm) minimum.

4.13.6 Maneuvering Clearances at Doors. Minimum maneuvering clearances at doors that are not automatic or power-assisted shall be as shown in Fig. 25. The floor or ground area within the required clearances shall be level and clear.
EXCEPTION: Entry doors to acute care hospital bedrooms for in-patients shall be exempted from the requirement for space at the latch side of the door (see dimension "x" in Fig. 25) if the door is at least 44 in (1120 mm) wide.

4.13.7 Two Doors in Series. The minimum space between two hinged or pivoted doors in series shall be 48 in (1220 mm) plus the width of any door swinging into the space. Doors in series shall swing either in the same direction or away from the space between the doors (see Fig. 26).

4.13.8* Thresholds at Doorways. Thresholds at doorways shall not exceed 3/4 in (19 mm) in height for exterior sliding doors or 1/2 in (13 mm) for other types of doors. Raised thresholds and floor level changes at accessible doorways shall be beveled with a slope no greater than 1:2 (see 4.5.2).

4.13.9* Door Hardware. Handles, pulls, latches, locks, and other operating devices on accessible doors shall have a shape that is easy to grasp with one hand and does not require tight grasping, tight pinching, or twisting of the wrist to operate. Lever-operated mechanisms, push-type mechanisms, and U-shaped handles are acceptable designs. When sliding doors are fully open operating hardware shall be exposed and usable from both sides. Hardware required for accessible door passage shall be mounted no higher than 48 in (1220 mm) above finished floor.

4.13.10* Door Closers. If a door has a closer, then the sweep period of the closer shall be adjusted so that from an open position of 70 degrees, the door will take at least 3 seconds to move to a point 3 in (75 mm) from the latch, measured to the leading edge of the door.

4.13.11* Door Opening Force. The maximum force for pushing or pulling open a door shall be as follows:

(1) Fire doors shall have the minimum opening force allowable by the appropriate administrative authority.

(2) Other doors.

(a) exterior hinged doors: (Reserved).

(b) interior hinged doors: 5 lbf (22.2N)

(c) sliding or folding doors: 5 lbf (22.2N)
These forces do not apply to the force required to retract latch bolts or disengage other devices that may hold the door in a closed position.

4.13.12* Automatic Doors and Power-Assisted Doors. If an automatic door is used, then it shall comply with ANSI/BHMA A156.10-1985. Slowly opening, low-powered, automatic doors shall comply with ANSI A156.19-1984. Such doors shall not open to back check faster than 3 seconds and shall require no more than 15 lbf (66.6N) to stop door movement. If a power-assisted door is used, its door-opening force shall comply with 4.13.11 and its closing shall conform to the requirements in ANSI A156.19-1984.

4.14 Entrances.

4.14.1 Minimum Number. Entrances required to be accessible by 4.1 shall be part of an accessible route complying with 4.3. Such entrances shall be connected by an accessible route to public transportation stops, to accessible parking and passenger loading zones, and to public streets or sidewalks if available (see 4.3.2(1)). They shall also be connected by an accessible route to all accessible spaces or elements within the building or facility.

4.14.2 Service Entrances. A service entrance shall not be the sole accessible entrance unless it is the only entrance to a building or facility (for example, in a factory or garage).

4.15 Drinking Fountains and Water Coolers.

4.15.1 Minimum Number. Drinking fountains or water coolers required to be accessible by 4.1 shall comply with 4.15.

4.15.2* Spout Height. Spouts shall be no higher than 36 in (915 mm), measured from the floor or ground surfaces to the spout outlet (see Fig. 27(a)).

4.15.3 Spout Location. The spouts of drinking fountains and water coolers shall be at the front of the unit and shall direct the water flow in a trajectory that is parallel or nearly parallel to the front of the unit. The spout shall provide a flow of water at least 4 in (100 mm) high so as to allow the insertion of a cup or glass under the flow of water. On an accessible drinking fountain with a round or oval bowl, the spout must be positioned so the flow of water is within 3 in (75 mm) of the front edge of the fountain.

4.15.4 Controls. Controls shall comply with 4.27.4. Unit controls shall be front mounted or side mounted near the front edge.

4.15.5 Clearances.

(1) Wall- and post-mounted cantilevered units shall have a clear knee space between the bottom of the apron and the floor or ground at least 27 in (685 mm) high, 30 in (760 mm) wide, and 17 in to 19 in (430 mm to 485 mm) deep (see Fig. 27(a) and (b)). Such units shall also have a minimum clear floor space 30 in by 48 in (760 mm by 1220 mm) to allow a person in a wheelchair to approach the unit facing forward.

(2) Free-standing or built-in units not having a clear space under them shall have a clear floor space at least 30 in by 48 in (760 mm by 1220 mm) that allows a person in a wheelchair to make a parallel approach to the unit (see Fig. 27(c) and (d)). This clear floor space shall comply with 4.2.4.

4.16 Water Closets.

4.16.1 General. Accessible water closets shall comply with 4.16.

4.16.2 Clear Floor Space. Clear floor space for water closets not in stalls shall comply with Fig. 28. Clear floor space may be arranged to allow either a left-handed or right-handed approach.

4.16.3* Height. The height of water closets shall be 17 in to 19 in (430 mm to 485 mm), measured to the top of the toilet seat (see Fig. 29(b)). Seats shall not be sprung to return to a lifted position.

4.16.4* Grab Bars. Grab bars for water closets not located in stalls shall comply with 4.26 and Fig. 29. The grab bar behind the water closet shall be 36 in (915 mm) minimum.

4.16.5* Flush Controls. Flush controls shall be hand operated or automatic and shall comply with 4.27.4. Controls for flush valves shall be mounted on the wide side of toilet areas no more than 44 in (1120 mm) above the floor.

4.16.6 Dispensers. Toilet paper dispensers shall be installed within reach, as shown in Fig. 29(b). Dispensers that control delivery, or that do not permit continuous paper flow, shall not be used.

4.17 Toilet Stalls.

4.17.1 Location. Accessible toilet stalls shall be on an accessible route and shall meet the requirements of 4.17.

4.17.2 Water Closets. Water closets in accessible stalls shall comply with 4.16.

4.17.3* Size and Arrangement. The size and arrangement of the standard toilet stall shall comply with Fig. 30(a), Standard Stall. Standard toilet stalls with a minimum depth of 56 in (1420 mm) (see Fig. 30(a)) shall have wall-mounted water closets. If the depth of a standard toilet stall is increased at least 3 in (75 mm), then a floor-mounted water closet may be used. Arrangements shown for standard toilet stalls may be reversed to allow either a left- or right-hand approach. Additional stalls shall be provided in conformance with 4.22.4.

EXCEPTION: In instances of alteration work where provision of a standard stall (Fig. 30(a)) is technically infeasible or where plumbing code requirements prevent combining existing stalls to provide space, either alternate stall (Fig. 30(b)) may be provided in lieu of the standard stall.

4.17.4 Toe Clearances. In standard stalls, the front partition and at least one side partition shall provide a toe clearance of at least 9 in (230 mm) above the floor. If the depth of the stall is greater than 60 in (1525 mm), then the toe clearance is not required.

4.17.5* Doors. Toilet stall doors, including door hardware, shall comply with 4.13. If toilet stall approach is from the latch side of the stall door, clearance between the door side of the stall and any obstruction may be reduced to a minimum of 42 in (1065 mm) (Fig. 30).

4.17.6 Grab Bars. Grab bars complying with the length and positioning shown in Fig. 30(a), (b), (c), and (d) shall be provided. Grab bars may be mounted with any desired method as long as they have a gripping surface at the locations shown and do not obstruct the required clear floor area. Grab bars shall comply with 4.26.

4.18 Urinals.

4.18.1 General. Accessible urinals shall comply with 4.18.

4.18.2 Height. Urinals shall be stall-type or wall-hung with an elongated rim at a maximum of 17 in (430 mm) above the finish floor.

4.18.3 Clear Floor Space. A clear floor space 30 in by 48 in (760 mm by 1220 mm) shall be provided in front of urinals to allow forward approach. This clear space shall adjoin or overlap an accessible route and shall comply with 4.2.4. Urinal shields that do not extend beyond the front edge of the urinal rim may be provided with 29 in (735 mm) clearance between them.

4.18.4 Flush Controls. Flush controls shall be hand operated or automatic, and shall comply with 4.27.4, and shall be mounted no more than 44 in (1120 mm) above the finish floor.

4.19 Lavatories and Mirrors.

4.19.1 General. The requirements of 4.19 shall apply to lavatory fixtures, vanities, and built-in lavatories.

4.19.2 Height and Clearances. Lavatories shall be mounted with the rim or counter surface no higher than 34 in (865 mm) above the finish floor. Provide a clearance of at least 29 in (735 mm) above the finish floor to the bottom of the apron. Knee and toe clearance shall comply with Fig. 31.

4.19.3 Clear Floor Space. A clear floor space 30 in by 48 in (760 mm by 1220 mm) complying with 4.2.4 shall be provided in front of a lavatory to allow forward approach. Such clear floor space shall adjoin or overlap an accessible route and shall extend a maximum of 19 in (485 mm) underneath the lavatory (see Fig. 32).

4.19.4 Exposed Pipes and Surfaces. Hot water and drain pipes under lavatories shall be insulated or otherwise configured to protect against contact. There shall be no sharp or abrasive surfaces under lavatories.

4.19.5 Faucets. Faucets shall comply with 4.27.4. Lever-operated, push-type, and electronically controlled mechanisms are examples of acceptable designs. If self-closing valves are used the faucet shall remain open for at least 10 seconds.

4.19.6* Mirrors. Mirrors shall be mounted with the bottom edge of the reflecting surface no higher than 40 in (1015 mm) above the finish floor (see Fig. 31).

4.20 Bathtubs.

4.20.1 General. Accessible bathtubs shall comply with 4.20.

4.20.2 Floor Space. Clear floor space in front of bathtubs shall be as shown in Fig. 33.

4.20.3 Seat. An in-tub seat or a seat at the head end of the tub shall be provided as shown in Fig. 33 and 34. The structural strength of seats and their attachments shall comply with 4.26.3. Seats shall be mounted securely and shall not slip during use.

4.20.4 Grab Bars. Grab bars complying with 4.26 shall be provided as shown in Fig. 33 and 34.

4.20.5 Controls. Faucets and other controls complying with 4.27.4 shall be located as shown in Fig. 34.

4.20.6 Shower Unit. A shower spray unit with a hose at least 60 in (1525 mm) long that can be used both as a fixed shower head and as a hand-held shower shall be provided.

4.20.7 Bathtub Enclosures. If provided, enclosures for bathtubs shall not obstruct controls or transfer from wheelchairs onto bathtub seats or into tubs. Enclosures on bathtubs shall not have tracks mounted on their rims.

4.21 Shower Stalls.

4.21.1* General. Accessible shower stalls shall comply with 4.21.

4.21.2 Size and Clearances. Except as specified in 9.1.2, showerstall size and clear floor space shall comply with Fig. 35(a) or (b). The shower stall in Fig. 35(a) shall be 36 in by 36 in (915 mm by 915 mm). Shower stalls required by 9.1.2 shall comply with Fig. 57(a) or (b). The shower stall in Fig. 35(b) will fit into the space required for a bathtub.

4.21.3 Seat. A seat shall be provided in shower stalls 36 in by 36 in (915 mm by 915 mm) and shall be as shown in Fig. 36. The seat shall be mounted 17 in to 19 in (430 mm to 485 mm) from the bathroom floor and shall extend the full depth of the stall. In a 36 in by 36 in (915 mm by 915 mm) shower stall, the seat shall be on the wall opposite the controls. Where a fixed seat is provided in a 30 in by 60 in minimum (760 mm by 1525 mm) shower stall, it shall be a folding type and shall be mounted on the wall adjacent to the controls as shown in Fig. 57. The structural strength of seats and their attachments shall comply with 4.26.3.

4.21.4 Grab Bars. Grab bars complying with 4.26 shall be provided as shown in Fig. 37.

4.21.5 Controls. Faucets and other controls complying with 4.27.4 shall be located as shown in Fig. 37. In shower stalls 36 in by 36 in (915 mm by 915 mm), all controls, faucets, and the shower unit shall be mounted on the side wall opposite the seat.

4.21.6 Shower Unit. A shower spray unit with a hose at least 60 in (1525 mm) long that can be used both as a fixed shower head and as a hand-held shower shall be provided.

EXCEPTION: In unmonitored facilities where vandalism is a consideration, a fixed shower head mounted at 48 in (1220 mm) above the shower floor may be used in lieu of a hand-held shower head.

4.21.7 Curbs. If provided, curbs in shower stalls 36 in by 36 in (915 mm by 915 mm) shall be no higher than 1/2 in (13 mm). Shower stalls that are 30 in by 60 in (760 mm by 1525 mm) minimum shall not have curbs.

4.21.8 Shower Enclosures. If provided, enclosures for shower stalls shall not obstruct controls or obstruct transfer from wheelchairs onto shower seats.

4.22 Toilet Rooms.

4.22.1 Minimum Number. Toilet facilities required to be accessible by 4.1 shall comply with 4.22. Accessible toilet rooms shall be on an accessible route.

4.22.2 Doors. All doors to accessible toilet rooms shall comply with 4.13. Doors shall not swing into the clear floor space required for any fixture.

4.22.3* Clear Floor Space. The accessible fixtures and controls required in 4.22.4, 4.22.5, 4.22.6, and 4.22.7 shall be on an accessible route. An unobstructed turning space complying with 4.2.3 shall be provided within an accessible toilet room. The clear floor space at fixtures and controls, the accessible route, and the turning space may overlap.

4.22.4 Water Closets. If toilet stalls are provided, then at least one shall be a standard toilet stall complying with 4.17; where 6 or more stalls are provided, in addition to the stall complying with 4.17.3, at least one stall 36 in (915 mm) wide with an outward swinging, self-closing door and parallel grab bars complying with Fig. 30(d) and 4.26 shall be provided. Water closets in such stalls shall comply with 4.16. If water closets are not in stalls, then at least one shall comply with 4.16.

4.22.5 Urinals. If urinals are provided, then at least one shall comply with 4.18.

4.22.6 Lavatories and Mirrors. If lavatories and mirrors are provided, then at least one of each shall comply with 4.19.

4.22.7 Controls and Dispensers. If controls, dispensers, receptacles, or other equipment are provided, then at least one of each shall be on an accessible route and shall comply with 4.27.

4.23 Bathrooms, Bathing Facilities, and Shower Rooms.

4.23.1 Minimum Number. Bathrooms, bathing facilities, or shower rooms required to be accessible by 4.1 shall comply with 4.23 and shall be on an accessible route.

4.23.2 Doors. Doors to accessible bathrooms shall comply with 4.13. Doors shall not swing into the floor space required for any fixture.

4.23.3* Clear Floor Space. The accessible fixtures and controls required in 4.23.4, 4.23.5, 4.23.6, 4.23.7, 4.23.8, and 4.23.9 shall be on an accessible route. An unobstructed turning space complying with 4.2.3 shall be provided within an accessible bathroom. The clear floor spaces at fixtures and controls, the accessible route, and the turning space may overlap.

4.23.4 Water Closets. If toilet stalls are provided, then at least one shall be a standard toilet stall complying with 4.17; where 6 or more stalls are provided, in addition to the stall complying with 4.17.3, at least one stall 36 in (915 mm) wide with an outward swinging, self-closing door and parallel grab bars complying with Fig. 30(d) and 4.26 shall be provided. Water closets in such stalls shall comply with 4.16. If water closets are not in stalls, then at least one shall comply with 4.16.

4.23.5 Urinals. If urinals are provided, then at least one shall comply with 4.18.

4.23.6 Lavatories and Mirrors. If lavatories and mirrors are provided, then at least one of each shall comply with 4.19.

4.23.7 Controls and Dispensers. If controls, dispensers, receptacles, or other equipment are provided, then at least one of each shall be on an accessible route and shall comply with 4.27.

4.23.8 Bathing and Shower Facilities. If tubs or showers are provided, then at least one accessible tub that complies with 4.20 or at least one accessible shower that complies with 4.21 shall be provided.

4.23.9* Medicine Cabinets. If medicine cabinets are provided, at least one shall be located with a usable shelf no higher than 44 in (1120 mm) above the floor space. The floor space shall comply with 4.2.4.

4.24 Sinks.

4.24.1 General. Sinks required to be accessible by 4.1 shall comply with 4.24.

4.24.2 Height. Sinks shall be mounted with the counter or rim no higher than 34 in (865 mm) above the finish floor.

4.24.3 Knee Clearance. Knee clearance that is at least 27 in (685 mm) high, 30 in (760 mm) wide, and 19 in (485 mm) deep shall be provided underneath sinks.

4.24.4 Depth. Each sink shall be a maximum of 6-1/2 in (165 mm) deep.

4.24.5 Clear Floor Space. A clear floor space at least 30 in by 48 in (760 mm by 1220 mm) complying with 4.2.4 shall be provided in front of a sink to allow forward approach. The clear floor space shall be on an accessible route and shall extend a maximum of 19 in (485 mm) underneath the sink (see Fig. 32).

4.24.6 Exposed Pipes and Surfaces Hot water and drain pipes exposed under sinks shall be insulated or otherwise configured so as to protect against contact. There shall be no sharp or abrasive surfaces under sinks.

4.24.7 Faucets. Faucets shall comply with 4.27.4. Lever-operated, push-type, touch-type, or electronically controlled mechanisms are acceptable designs.

4.25 Storage.

4.25.1 General. Fixed storage facilities such as cabinets, shelves, closets, and drawers required to be accessible by 4.1 shall comply with 4.25.

4.25.2 Clear Floor Space. A clear floor space at least 30 in by 48 in (760 mm by 1220 mm) complying with 4.2.4 that allows either a forward or parallel approach by a person using a wheelchair shall be provided at accessible storage facilities.

4.25.3 Height. Accessible storage spaces shall be within at least one of the reach ranges specified in 4.2.5 and 4.2.6 (see Fig. 5 and Fig 6). Clothes rods or shelves shall be a maximum of 54 in (1370 mm) above the finish floor for a side approach. Where the distance from the wheelchair to the clothes rod or shelf exceeds 10 in (255 mm) (as in closets without accessible doors) the height and depth to the rod or shelf shall comply with Fig. 38(a) and Fig. 38(b).

4.25.4 Hardware. Hardware for accessible storage facilities shall comply with 4.27.4. Touch latches and U-shaped pulls are acceptable.

4.26 Handrails, Grab Bars, and Tub and Shower Seats.

4.26.1* General. All handrails, grab bars, and tub and shower seats required to be accessible by 4.1, 4.8, 4.9, 4.16, 4.17, 4.20 or 4.21 shall comply with 4.26.

4.26.2* Size and Spacing of Grab Bars and Handrails. The diameter or width of the gripping surfaces of a handrail or grab bar shall be 1-1/4 in to 1-1/2 in (32 mm to 38 mm), or the shape shall provide an equivalent gripping surface. If handrails or grab bars are mounted adjacent to a wall, the space between the wall and the grab bar shall be 1-1/2 in (38 mm) (see Fig. 39(a), (b), (c), and (e)). Handrails may be located in a recess if the recess is a maximum of 3 in (75 mm) deep and extends at least 18 in (455 mm) above the top of the rail (see Fig. 39(d)).

4.26.3 Structural Strength. The structural strength of grab bars, tub and shower seats, fasteners, and mounting devices shall meet the following specification:

(1) Bending stress in a grab bar or seat induced by the maximum bending moment from the application of 250 lbf (1112N) shall be less than the allowable stress for the material of the grab bar or seat.

(2) Shear stress induced in a grab bar or seat by the application of 250 lbf (1112N) shall be less than the allowable shear stress for the material of the grab bar or seat. If the connection between the grab bar or seat and its mounting bracket or other support is considered to be fully restrained, then direct and torsional shear stresses shall be totaled for the combined shear stress, which shall not exceed the allowable shear stress.

(3) Shear force induced in a fastener or mounting device from the application of 250 lbf (1112N) shall be less than the allowable lateral load of either the fastener or mounting device or the supporting structure, whichever is the smaller allowable load.

(4) Tensile force induced in a fastener by a direct tension force of 250 lbf (1112N) plus the maximum moment from the application of 250 lbf (1112N) shall be less than the allowable withdrawal load between the fastener and the supporting structure.

(5) Grab bars shall not rotate within their fittings.

4.26.4 Eliminating Hazards. A handrail or grab bar and any wall or other surface adjacent to it shall be free of any sharp or abrasive elements. Edges shall have a minimum radius of 1/8 in (3.2 mm).

4.27 Controls and Operating Mechanisms.

4.27.1 General. Controls and operating mechanisms required to be accessible by 4.1 shall comply with 4.27.

4.27.2 Clear Floor Space. Clear floor space complying with 4.2.4 that allows a forward or a parallel approach by a person using a wheelchair shall be provided at controls, dispensers, receptacles, and other operable equipment.

4.27.3* Height. The highest operable part of controls, dispensers, receptacles, and other operable equipment shall be placed within at least one of the reach ranges specified in 4.2.5 and 4.2.6. Electrical and communications system receptacles on walls shall be mounted no less than 15 in (380 mm) above the floor.

EXCEPTION: These requirements do not apply where the use of special equipment dictates otherwise or where electrical and communications systems receptacles are not normally intended for use by building occupants.

4.27.4 Operation. Controls and operating mechanisms shall be operable with one hand and shall not require tight grasping, pinching, or twisting of the wrist. The force required to activate controls shall be no greater than 5 lbf (22.2 N).

4.28 Alarms.

4.28.1 General. Alarm systems required to be accessible by 4.1 shall comply with 4.28. At a minimum, visual signal appliances shall be provided in buildings and facilities in each of the following areas: restrooms and any other general usage areas (e.g., meeting rooms), hallways, lobbies, and any other area for common use.

4.28.2* Audible Alarms. If provided, audible emergency alarms shall produce a sound that exceeds the prevailing equivalent sound level in the room or space by at least 15 dbA or exceeds any maximum sound level with a duration of 60 seconds by 5 dbA, whichever is louder. Sound levels for alarm signals shall not exceed 120 dbA.

4.28.3* Visual Alarms. Visual alarm signal appliances shall be integrated into the building or facility alarm system. If single station audible alarms are provided then single station visual alarm signals shall be provided. Visual alarm signals shall have the following minimum photometric and location features:

(1) The lamp shall be a xenon strobe type or equivalent.

(2) The color shall be clear or nominal white (i.e., unfiltered or clear filtered white light).

(3) The maximum pulse duration shall be two-tenths of one second (0.2 sec) with a maximum duty cycle of 40 percent. The pulse duration is defined as the time interval between initial and final points of 10 percent of maximum signal.

(4) The intensity shall be a minimum of 75 candela.

(5) The flash rate shall be a minimum of 1 Hz and a maximum of 3 Hz.

(6) The appliance shall be placed 80 in (2030 mm) above the highest floor level within the space or 6 in (152 mm) below the ceiling, whichever is lower.

(7) In general, no place in any room or space required to have a visual signal appliance shall be more than 50 ft (15 m) from the signal (in the horizontal plane). In large rooms and spaces exceeding 100 ft (30 m) across, without obstructions 6 ft (2 m) above the finish floor, such as auditoriums, devices may be placed around the perimeter, spaced a maximum 100 ft (30 m) apart, in lieu of suspending appliances from the ceiling.

(8) No place in common corridors or hallways in which visual alarm signaling appliances are required shall be more than 50 ft (15 m) from the signal.

4.28.4* Auxiliary Alarms. Units and sleeping accommodations shall have a visual alarm connected to the building emergency alarm system or shall have a standard 110-volt electrical receptacle into which such an alarm can be connected and a means by which a signal from the building emergency alarm system can trigger such an auxiliary alarm. When visual alarms are in place the signal shall be visible in all areas of the unit or room. Instructions for use of the auxiliary alarm or receptacle shall be provided.

Requirements for detectable warnings at curb ramps, hazardous vehicular areas, and reflecting pools have been suspended until July 26, 1998. By that date, the ATBCB should issue a joint rule with the Departments of Justice and Transportation with respect to the need for and usability of the need for and usability of current technical specifications for detectable warnings at curb ramps, hazardous vehicular areas, and reflecting pools.

4.29 Detectable Warnings.

4.29.1 General. Detectable warnings required by 4.1 and 4.7 shall comply with 4.29.

4.29.2* Detectable Warnings on Walking Surfaces. Detectable warnings shall consist of raised truncated domes with a diameter of nominal 0.9 in (23 mm), a height of nominal 0.2 in (5 mm) and a center-to-center spacing of nominal 2.35 in (60 mm) and shall contrast visually with adjoining surfaces, either light-on-dark, or dark-on-light.

The material used to provide contrast shall be an integral part of the walking surface. Detectable warnings used on interior surfaces shall differ from adjoining walking surfaces in resiliency or sound-on-cane contact.

4.29.3 Detectable Warnings on Doors To Hazardous Areas. (Reserved).

4.29.4 Detectable Warnings at Stairs. (Reserved).

4.29.5 Detectable Warnings at Hazardous Vehicular Areas.
[Provision suspended until July 26, 1998] If a walk crosses or
adjoins a vehicular way, and the walking surfaces are not
separated by curbs, railings, or other elements between the
pedestrian areas and vehicular areas, the boundary between the
areas shall be defined by a continuous detectable warning which
is 36 in (915 mm) wide, complying with 4.29.2.

4.29.6 Detectable Warnings at Reflecting Pools. [Provision
suspended until July 26, 1998] The edges of reflecting pools shall
be protected by railings, walls, curbs, or detectable warnings
complying with 4.29.2.

4.29.7 Standardization. (Reserved).

4.30 Signage.

4.30.1* General. Signage required to be accessible by 4.1 shall
comply with the applicable provisions of 4.30.

4.30.2* Character Proportion. Letters and numbers on signs
shall have a width-to-height ratio between 3:5 and 1:1 and a
stroke-width-to-height ratio between 1:5 and 1:10.

4.30.3 Character Height. Characters and numbers on signs
shall be sized according to the viewing distance from which they
are to be read. The minimum height is measured using an upper
case X. Lower case characters are permitted.

Height Above Finished Floor	Minimum Character Height
Suspended or Projected Overhead in compliance with 4.4.2	3 in (75 mm) minimum

**4.30.4* Raised and Brailled Characters and Pictorial Symbol
Signs (Pictograms)**. Letters and numerals shall be raised 1/32
in (0.8 mm) minimum, upper case, sans serif or simple serif type
and shall be accompanied with Grade 2 Braille. Raised
characters shall be at least 5/8 in (16 mm) high, but no higher
than 2 in (50 mm). Pictograms shall be accompanied by the
equivalent verbal description placed directly below the pictogram.
The border dimension of the pictogram shall be 6 in (152 mm)
minimum in height.

4.30.5* Finish and Contrast. The characters and background of
signs shall be eggshell, matte, or other non-glare finish.
Characters and symbols shall contrast with their background --
either light characters on a dark background or dark characters on
a light background.

4.30.6 Mounting Location and Height. Where permanent
identification is provided for rooms and spaces, signs shall be
installed on the wall adjacent to the latch side of the door.
Where there is no wall space to the latch side of the door,
including at double leaf doors, signs shall be placed on the
nearest adjacent wall. Mounting height shall be 60 in (1525 mm)
above the finish floor to the centerline of the sign. Mounting
location for such signage shall be so that a person may approach
within 3 in (76 mm) of signage without encountering protruding
objects or standing within the swing of a door.

4.30.7* Symbols of Accessibility.

(1) Facilities and elements required to be identified as accessible by 4.1 shall use the international symbol of accessibility. The symbol shall be displayed as shown in Fig. 43(a) and (b).

(2) Volume Control Telephones. Telephones required to have a volume control by 4.1.3(17)(b) shall be identified by a sign containing a depiction of a telephone handset with radiating sound waves.

(3) Text Telephones. Text telephones required by 4.1.3(17)(c) shall be identified by the international TDD symbol (Fig 43(c)). In addition, if a facility has a public text telephone, directional signage indicating the location of the nearest text telephone shall be placed adjacent to all banks of telephones which do not contain a text telephone. Such directional signage shall include the international TDD symbol. If a facility has no banks of telephones, the directional signage shall be provided at the entrance (e.g., in a building directory).

(4) Assistive Listening Systems. In assembly areas where permanently installed assistive listening systems are required by 4.1.3(19)(b) the availability of such systems shall be identified with signage that includes the international symbol of access for hearing loss (Fig 43(d)).

4.30.8* Illumination Levels. (Reserved).

4.31 Telephones.

4.31.1 General. Public telephones required to be accessible by 4.1 shall comply with 4.31.

4.31.2 Clear Floor or Ground Space. A clear floor or ground space at least 30 in by 48 in (760 mm by 1220 mm) that allows either a forward or parallel approach by a person using a wheelchair shall be provided at telephones (see Fig. 44). The clear floor or ground space shall comply with 4.2.4. Bases, enclosures, and fixed seats shall not impede approaches to telephones by people who use wheelchairs.

4.31.3* Mounting Height. The highest operable part of the telephone shall be within the reach ranges specified in 4.2.5 or 4.2.6.

4.31.4 Protruding Objects. Telephones shall comply with 4.4.

4.31.5 Hearing Aid Compatible and Volume Control Telephones Required by 4.1.

(1) Telephones shall be hearing aid compatible.

(2) Volume controls, capable of a minimum of 12 dbA and a maximum of 18 dbA above normal, shall be provided in accordance with 4.1.3. If an automatic reset is provided then 18 dbA may be exceeded.

4.31.6 Controls. Telephones shall have pushbutton controls where service for such equipment is available.

4.31.7 Telephone Books. Telephone books, if provided, shall be located in a position that complies with the reach ranges specified in 4.2.5 and 4.2.6.

4.31.8 Cord Length. The cord from the telephone to the handset shall be at least 29 in (735 mm) long.

4.31.9* Text Telephones Required by 4.1.

(1) Text telephones used with a pay telephone shall be permanently affixed within, or adjacent to, the telephone enclosure. If an acoustic coupler is used, the telephone cord shall be sufficiently long to allow connection of the text telephone and the telephone receiver.

(2) Pay telephones designed to accommodate a portable text telephone shall be equipped with a shelf and an electrical outlet within or adjacent to the telephone enclosure. The telephone handset shall be capable of being placed flush on the surface of the shelf. The shelf shall be capable of accommodating a text telephone and shall have 6 in (152 mm) minimum vertical clearance in the area where the text telephone is to be placed.

(3) Equivalent facilitation may be provided. For example, a portable text telephone may be made available in a hotel at the registration desk if it is available on a 24-hour basis for use with nearby public pay telephones. In this instance, at least one pay telephone shall comply with paragraph 2 of this section. In addition, if an acoustic coupler is used, the telephone handset cord shall be sufficiently long so as to allow connection of the text telephone and the telephone receiver. Directional signage shall be provided and shall comply with 4.30.7.

4.32 Fixed or Built-in Seating and Tables.

4.32.1 Minimum Number. Fixed or built-in seating or tables required to be accessible by 4.1 shall comply with 4.32.

4.32.2 Seating. If seating spaces for people in wheelchairs are provided at fixed tables or counters, clear floor space complying with 4.2.4 shall be provided. Such clear floor space shall not overlap knee space by more than 19 in (485 mm) (see Fig. 45).

4.32.3 Knee Clearances. If seating for people in wheelchairs is provided at tables or counters, knee spaces at least 27 in (685 mm) high, 30 in (760 mm) wide, and 19 in (485 mm) deep shall be provided (see Fig. 45).

4.32.4* Height of Tables or Counters. The tops of accessible tables and counters shall be from 28 in to 34 in (710 mm to 865 mm) above the finish floor or ground.

4.33 Assembly Areas.

4.33.1 Minimum Number. Assembly and associated areas required to be accessible by 4.1 shall comply with 4.33.

4.33.2* Size of Wheelchair Locations. Each wheelchair location shall provide minimum clear ground or floor spaces as shown in Fig. 46.

4.33.3* Placement of Wheelchair Locations. Wheelchair areas shall be an integral part of any fixed seating plan and shall be provided so as to provide people with physical disabilities a choice of admission prices and lines of sight comparable to those for members of the general public. They shall adjoin an accessible route that also serves as a means of egress in case of emergency. At least one companion fixed seat shall be provided next to each wheelchair seating area. When the seating capacity exceeds 300, wheelchair spaces shall be provided in more than one location. Readily removable seats may be installed in wheelchair spaces when the spaces are not required to accommodate wheelchair users.

EXCEPTION: Accessible viewing positions may be clustered for bleachers, balconies, and other areas having sight lines that require slopes of greater than 5 percent. Equivalent accessible viewing positions may be located on levels having accessible egress.

4.33.4 Surfaces. The ground or floor at wheelchair locations shall be level and shall comply with 4.5.

4.33.5 Access to Performing Areas. An accessible route shall connect wheelchair seating locations with performing areas, including stages, arena floors, dressing rooms, locker rooms, and other spaces used by performers.

4.33.6* Placement of Listening Systems. If the listening system provided serves individual fixed seats, then such seats shall be located within a 50 ft (15 m) viewing distance of the stage or playing area and shall have a complete view of the stage or playing area.

4.33.7* Types of Listening Systems. Assistive listening systems (ALS) are intended to augment standard public address and audio systems by providing signals which can be received directly by persons with special receivers or their own hearing aids and which eliminate or filter background noise. The type of assistive listening system appropriate for a particular application depends on the characteristics of the setting, the nature of the program, and the intended audience. Magnetic induction loops, infra-red and radio frequency systems are types of listening systems which are appropriate for various applications.

4.34 Automated Teller Machines.

4.34.1 General. Each automated teller machine required to be accessible by 4.1.3 shall be on an accessible route and shall comply with 4.34

4.34.2 Clear Floor Space. The automated teller machine shall be located so that clear floor space complying with 4.2.4 is provided to allow a person using a wheelchair to make a forward approach, a parallel approach, or both, to the machine.

4.34.3 Reach Ranges

(1) Forward Approach Only. If only a forward approach is possible, operable parts of all controls shall be placed within the forward reach range specified in 4.2.5.

(2) Parallel Approach Only. If only a parallel approach is possible, operable parts of controls shall be placed as follows:

(a) Reach Depth Not More Than 10 In (255 Mm). Where the reach depth to the operable parts of all controls as measured from the vertical plane perpendicular to the edge of the unobstructed clear floor space at the farthest protrusion of the automated teller machine or surround is not more than 10 in (255 mm), the maximum height above the finished floor or grade shall be 54 in (1370 mm).

(b) Reach Depth More Than 10 In (255 Mm). Where the reach depth to the operable parts of any control as measured from the vertical plane perpendicular to the edge of the unobstructed clear floor space at the farthest protrusion of the automated teller machine or surround is more than 10 in (255 mm), the maximum height above the finished floor or grade shall be as follows:

Reach Depth		Maximum Height	
In	Mm	In	Mm
10	255	54	1370
11	280	53 1/2	1360
12	305	53	1345
13	330	52 1/2	1335
14	355	51 1/2	1310
15	380	51	1295
16	405	50 1/2	1285
17	430	50	1270
18	455	49 1/2	1255
19	485	49	1245
20	510	48 1/2	1230
21	535	47 1/2	1205
22	560	47	1195
23	585	46 1/2	1180
24	610	46	1170

(3) Forward and Parallel Approach. If both a forward and parallel approach are possible, operable parts of controls shall be placed within at least one of the reach ranges in paragraphs (1) or (2) of this section.

(4) Bins. Where bins are provided for envelopes, waste paper, or other purposes, at least one of each type provided shall comply with the applicable reach ranges in paragraph (1), (2), or (3) of this section.

EXCEPTION: Where a function can be performed in a substantially equivalent manner by using an alternate control, only one of the controls needed to perform that function is required to comply with this section. If the controls are identified by tactile markings, such markings shall be provided on both controls.

4.34.4 Controls. Controls for user activation shall comply with 4.27.4.

4.34.5 Equipment for Persons with Vision Impairments. Instructions and all information for use shall be made accessible to and independently usable by persons with vision impairments.

4.35 Dressing and Fitting Rooms.

4.35.1 General. Dressing and fitting rooms required to be accessible by 4.1 shall comply with 4.35 and shall be on an accessible route.

4.35.2 Clear Floor Space. A clear floor space allowing a person using a wheelchair to make a 180-degree turn shall be provided in every accessible dressing room entered through a swinging or sliding door. No door shall swing into any part of the turning space. Turning space shall not be required in a private dressing room entered through a curtained opening at least 32 in (815 mm) wide if clear floor space complying with section 4.2 renders the dressing room usable by a person using a wheelchair.

4.35.3 Doors. All doors to accessible dressing rooms shall be in compliance with section 4.13.

4.35.4 Bench. Every accessible dressing room shall have a 24 in by 48 in (610 mm by 1220 mm) bench fixed to the wall along the longer dimension. The bench shall be mounted 17 in to 19 in (430 mm to 485 mm) above the finish floor. Clear floor space shall be provided alongside the bench to allow a person using a wheelchair to make a parallel transfer onto the bench. The structural strength of the bench and attachments shall comply with 4.26.3. Where installed in conjunction with showers, swimming pools, or other wet locations, water shall not accumulate upon the surface of the bench and the bench shall have a slip-resistant surface.

4.35.5 Mirror. Where mirrors are provided in dressing rooms of the same use, then in an accessible dressing room, a full-length mirror, measuring at least 18 in wide by 54 in high (460 mm by 1370 mm), shall be mounted in a position affording a view to a person on the bench as well as to a person in a standing position.

NOTE: Sections 4.1.1 through 4.1.7 and sections 5 through 10 are different from ANSI A117.1 in their entirety and are printed in standard type.

5. RESTAURANTS AND CAFETERIAS.

5.1* General. Except as specified or modified in this section, restaurants and cafeterias shall comply with the requirements of 4.1 to 4.35. Where fixed tables (or dining counters where food is consumed but there is no service) are provided, at least 5 percent, but not less than one, of the fixed tables (or a portion of the dining counter) shall be accessible and shall comply with 4.32 as required in 4.1.3(18). In establishments where separate areas are designated for smoking and non-smoking patrons, the required number of accessible fixed tables (or counters) shall be proportionally distributed between the smoking and non-smoking areas. In new construction, and where practicable in alterations, accessible fixed tables (or counters) shall be distributed throughout the space or facility.

5.2 Counters and Bars. Where food or drink is served at counters exceeding 34 in (865 mm) in height for consumption by customers seated on stools or standing at the counter, a portion of the main counter which is 60 in (1525 mm) in length minimum shall be provided in compliance with 4.32 or service shall be available at accessible tables within the same area.

5.3 Access Aisles. All accessible fixed tables shall be accessibility by means of an access aisle at least 36 in (915 mm) clear between parallel edges of tables or between a wall and the table edges.

5.4 Dining Areas. In new construction, all dining areas, including raised or sunken dining areas, loggias, and outdoor seating areas, shall be accessible. In non-elevator buildings, an accessible means of vertical access to the mezzanine is not required under the following conditions: 1) the area of mezzanine seating measures no more than 33 percent of the area of the total accessible seating area; 2) the same services and decor are provided in an accessible space usable by the general public; and, 3) the accessible areas are not restricted to use by people with disabilities. In alterations, accessibility to raised or sunken dining areas, or to all parts of outdoor seating areas is not required provided that the same services and decor are provided in an accessible space usable by the general public and are not restricted to use by people with disabilities.

5.5 Food Service Lines. Food service lines shall have a minimum clear width of 36 in (915 mm), with a preferred clear width of 42 in (1065 mm) to allow passage around a person using a wheelchair. Tray slides shall be mounted no higher than 34 in (865 mm) above the floor (see Fig. 53). If self-service shelves are provided, at least 50 percent of each type must be within reach ranges specified in 4.2.5 and 4.2.6.

5.6 Tableware and Condiment Areas. Self-service shelves and dispensing devices for tableware, dishware, condiments, food and beverages shall be installed to comply with 4.2 (see Fig. 54).

5.7 Raised Platforms. In banquet rooms or spaces where a head table or speaker's lectern is located on a raised platform, the platform shall be accessible in compliance with 4.8 or 4.11. Open edges of a raised platform shall be protected by placement of tables or by a curb.

5.8 Vending Machines and Other Equipment. Spaces for vending machines and other equipment shall comply with 4.2 and shall be located on an accessible route.

5.9 Quiet Areas. (Reserved).

6. MEDICAL CARE FACILITIES.

6.1 General. Medical care facilities included in this section are those in which people receive physical or medical treatment or care and where persons may need assistance in responding to an emergency and where the period of stay may exceed twenty-four hours. In addition to the requirements of 4.1 through 4.35. medical care facilities and buildings shall comply with 6.
(1) Hospitals - general purpose hospitals, psychiatric facilities, detoxification facilities - At least 10 percent of patient bedrooms and toilets, and all public use and common use areas are required to be designed and constructed to be accessible.

(2) Hospitals and rehabilitation facilities that specialize in treating conditions that affect mobility, or units within either that specialize in treating conditions that affect mobility - All patient bedrooms and toilets, and all public use and common use areas are required to be designed and constructed to be accessible.

(3) Long term care facilities, nursing homes - At least 50 percent of patient bedrooms and toilets, and all public use and common use areas are required to be designed and constructed to be accessible.

(4) Alterations to patient bedrooms.

(a) When patient bedrooms are being added or altered as part of a planned renovation of an entire wing, a department, or other discrete area of an existing medical facility, a percentage of the patient bedrooms that are being added or altered shall comply with 6.3. The percentage of accessible rooms provided shall be consistent with the percentage of rooms required to be accessible by the applicable requirements of 6.1(1), 6.1(2), or 6.1(3), until the number of accessible patient bedrooms in the facility equals the overall number that would be required if the facility were newly constructed. (For example, if 20 patient bedrooms are being altered in the obstetrics department of a hospital, 2 of the altered rooms must be made accessible. If, within the same hospital, 20 patient bedrooms are being altered in a unit that specializes in treating mobility impairments, all of the altered rooms must be made accessible.) Where toilet/bathrooms are part of patient bedrooms which are added or altered and required to be accessible, each such patient toilet/bathroom shall comply with 6.4.

(b) When patient bedrooms are being added or altered individually, and not as part of an alteration of the entire area, the altered patient bedrooms shall comply with 6.3, unless either: a) the number of accessible rooms provided in the department or area containing the altered patient bedroom equals the number of accessible patient bedrooms that would be required if the percentage requirements of 6.1(1), 6.1(2), or 6.1(3) were applied to that department or area; or b) the number of accessible patient bedrooms in the facility equals the overall number that would be required if the facility were newly constructed. Where toilet/bathrooms are part of patient bedrooms which are added or altered and required to be accessible, each such toilet/bathroom shall comply with 6.4.

6.2 Entrances. At least one accessible entrance that complies with 4.14 shall be protected from the weather by canopy or roof overhang. Such entrances shall incorporate a passenger loading zone that complies with 4.6.6.

6.3 Patient Bedrooms. Provide accessible patient bedrooms in compliance with 4.1 through 4.35. Accessible patient bedrooms shall comply with the following:
(1) Each bedroom shall have a door that complies with 4.13.

EXCEPTION: Entry doors to acute care hospital bedrooms for in-patients shall be exempted from the requirement in 4.13.6 for maneuvering space at the latch side of the door if the door is at least 44 in (1120 mm) wide.

(2) Each bedroom shall have adequate space to provide a maneuvering space that complies with 4.2.3. In rooms with 2 beds, it is preferable that this space be located between beds.

(3) Each bedroom shall have adequate space to provide a minimum clear floor space of 36 in (915 mm) along each side of the bed and to provide an accessible route complying with 4.3.3 to each side of each bed.

6.4 Patient Toilet Rooms. Where toilet/bath rooms are provided as a part of a patient bedroom, each patient bedroom that is required to be accessible shall have an accessible toilet/bath room that complies with 4.22 or 4.23 and shall be on an accessible route.

7. BUSINESS AND MERCANTILE.

7.1 General. In addition to the requirements of 4.1 to 4.35, the design of all areas used for business transactions with the public shall comply with 7.

7.2 Sales and Service Counters, Teller Windows, Information Counters.

(1) In department stores and miscellaneous retail stores where counters have cash registers and are provided for sales or distribution of goods or services to the public, at least one of each type shall have a portion of the counter which is at least 36 in (915mm) in length with a maximum height of 36 in (915 mm) above the finish floor. It shall be on an accessible route complying with 4.3. The accessible counters must be dispersed throughout the building or facility. In alterations where it is technically infeasible to provide an accessible counter, an auxiliary counter meeting these requirements may be provided.

(2) At ticketing counters, teller stations in a bank, registration counters in hotels and motels, box office ticket counters, and other counters that may not have a cash register but at which goods or services are sold or distributed, either:

(i) a portion of the main counter which is a minimum of 36 in (915 mm) in length shall be provided with a maximum height of 36 in (915 mm); or

(ii) an auxiliary counter with a maximum height of 36 in (915 mm) in close proximity to the main counter shall be provided; or

(iii) equivalent facilitation shall be provided (e.g., at a hotel registration counter, equivalent facilitation might consist of: (1) provision of a folding shelf attached to the main counter on which an individual with disabilities can write, and (2) use of the space on the side of the counter or at the concierge desk, for handing materials back and forth).

All accessible sales and service counters shall be on an accessible route complying with 4.3.

(3)* Assistive Listening Devices. (Reserved)

7.3" Check-out Aisles.

(1) In new construction, accessible check-out aisles shall be provided in conformance with the table below:

Total Check-out Aisles of Each Design	Minimum Number of Accessible Check-out Aisles (of each design)
1 - 4	1
5 - 8	2
9 - 15	3
over 15	3, plus 20% of additional aisles.

EXCEPTION: In new construction, where the selling space is under 5000 square feet, only one check-out aisle is required to be accessible.

EXCEPTION: In alterations, at least one check-out aisle shall be accessible in facilities under 5000 square feet of selling space. In facilities of 5000 or more square feet of selling space, at least one of each design of check-out aisle shall be made accessible when altered until the number of accessible check-out aisles of each design equals the number required in new construction.

Examples of check-out aisles of different "design" include those which are specifically designed to serve different functions. Different "design" includes but is not limited to the following features - length of belt or no belt; or permanent signage designating the aisle as an express lane.

(2) Clear aisle width for accessible check-out aisles shall comply with 4.2.1 and maximum adjoining counter height shall not exceed 38 in (965 mm) above the finish floor. The top of the lip shall not exceed 40 in (1015 mm) above the finish floor.

(3) Signage identifying accessible check-out aisles shall comply with 4.30.7 and shall be mounted above the check-out aisle in the same location where the check-out number or type of check-out is displayed.

7.4 Security Bollards.

Any device used to prevent the removal of shopping carts from store premises shall not prevent access or egress to people in wheelchairs. An alternate entry that is equally convenient to that provided for the ambulatory population is acceptable.

8. LIBRARIES.

8.1 General.

In addition to the requirements of 4.1 to 4.35, the design of all public areas of a library shall comply with 8, including reading and study areas, stacks, reference rooms, reserve areas, and special facilities or collections.

8.2 Reading and Study Areas.

At least 5 percent or a minimum of one of each element of fixed seating, tables, or study carrels shall comply with 4.2 and 4.32. Clearances between fixed accessible tables and between study carrels shall comply with 4.3.

8.3 Check-Out Areas. At least one lane at each check-out area shall comply with 7.2(1). Any traffic control or book security gates or turnstiles shall comply with 4.13.

8.4 Card Catalogs and Magazine Displays. Minimum clear aisle space at card catalogs and magazine displays shall comply with Fig. 55. Maximum reach height shall comply with 4.2, with a height of 48 in (1220 mm) preferred irrespective of approach allowed.

8.5 Stacks. Minimum clear aisle width between stacks shall comply with 4.3, with a minimum clear aisle width of 42 in (1065 mm) preferred where possible. Shelf height in stack areas is unrestricted (see Fig. 56).

9. ACCESSIBLE TRANSIENT LODGING.

(1) Except as specified in the special technical provisions of this section, accessible transient lodging shall comply with the applicable requirements of 4.1 through 4.35. Transient lodging includes facilities or portions thereof used for sleeping accommodations, when not classed as a medical care facility.

9.1 Hotels, Motels, Inns, Boarding Houses, Dormitories, Resorts and Other Similar Places of Transient Lodging.

9.1.1 General. All public use and common use areas are required to be designed and constructed to comply with section 4 (Accessible Elements and Spaces: Scope and Technical Requirements).

EXCEPTION: Sections 9.1 through 9.4 do not apply to an establishment located within a building that contains not more than five rooms for rent or hire and that is actually occupied by the proprietor of such establishment as the residence of such proprietor.

9.1.2 Accessible Units, Sleeping Rooms, and Suites. Accessible sleeping rooms or suites that comply with the requirements of 9.2 (Requirements for Accessible Units, Sleeping Rooms, and Suites) shall be provided in conformance with the table below. In addition, in hotels, of 50 or more sleeping rooms or suites, additional accessible sleeping rooms or suites that include a roll- in shower shall also be provided in conformance with the table below. Such accommodations shall comply with the requirements of 9.2, 4.21, and Figure 57(a) or (b).

Number of Rooms	Accessible Rooms	Rooms with Roll-in Showers
1 to 25	1	
26 to 50	2	
51 to 75	3	1
76 to 100	4	1
101 to 150	5	2
151 to 200	6	2
201 to 300	7	3
301 to 400	8	4
401 to 500	9	4, plus one for each additional 100 over 400
501 to 1000	2% of total	
1001 and over	20 plus 1 for each 100 over 1000	

9.1.3 Sleeping Accommodations for Persons with Hearing Impairments. In addition to those accessible sleeping rooms and suites required by 9.1.2, sleeping rooms and suites that comply with 9.3 (Visual Alarms, Notification Devices, and Telephones) shall be provided in conformance with the following table:

Number of Elements	Accessible Elements
1 to 25	1
26 to 50	2
51 to 75	3
76 to 100	4
101 to 150	5
151 to 200	6
201 to 300	7
301 to 400	8
401 to 500	9
501 to 1000	2% of total
1001 and over	20 plus 1 for each 100 over 1000

9.1.4 Classes of Sleeping Accommodations.

(1) In order to provide persons with disabilities a range of options equivalent to those available to other persons served by the facility, sleeping rooms and suites required to be accessible by 9.1.2 shall be dispersed among the various classes of sleeping accommodations available to patrons of the place of transient lodging. Factors to be considered include room size, cost, amenities provided, and the number of beds provided.

(2) Equivalent Facilitation. For purposes of this section, it shall be deemed equivalent facilitation if the operator of a facility elects to limit construction of accessible rooms to those intended for multiple occupancy, provided that such rooms are made available at the cost of a single occupancy room to an individual with disabilities who requests a single-occupancy room.

9.1.5. Alterations to Accessible Units, Sleeping Rooms, and Suites. When sleeping rooms are being altered in an existing facility, or portion thereof, subject to the requirements of this section, at least one sleeping room or suite that complies with the requirements of 9.2 (Requirements for Accessible Units, Sleeping Rooms, and Suites) shall be provided for each 25 sleeping rooms, or fraction thereof, of rooms being altered until the number of such rooms provided equals the number required to be accessible with 9.1.2. In addition, at least one sleeping room or suite that complies with the requirements of 9.3 (Visual Alarms, Notification Devices, and Telephones) shall be provided for each 25 sleeping rooms, or fraction thereof, of rooms being altered until the number of such rooms equals the number required to be accessible by 9.1.3.

9.2 Requirements for Accessible Units, Sleeping Rooms and Suites.

9.2.1 General. Units, sleeping rooms, and suites required to be accessible by 9.1 shall comply with 9.2.

9.2.2 Minimum Requirements. An accessible unit, sleeping room or suite shall be on an accessible route complying with 4.3

and have the following accessible elements and spaces.

(1) Accessible sleeping rooms shall have a 36 in (915 mm) clear width maneuvering space located along both sides of a bed, except that where two beds are provided, this requirement can be met by providing a 36 in (915 mm) wide maneuvering space located between the two beds.

(2) An accessible route complying with 4.3 shall connect all accessible spaces and elements, including telephones, within the unit, sleeping room, or suite. This is not intended to require an elevator in multi-story units as long as the spaces identified in 9.2.2(6) and (7) are on accessible levels and the accessible sleeping area is suitable for dual occupancy.

(3) Doors and doorways designed to allow passage into and within all sleeping rooms, suites or other covered units shall comply with 4.13.

(4) If fixed or built-in storage facilities such as cabinets, shelves, closets, and drawers are provided in accessible spaces, at least one of each type provided shall contain storage space complying with 4.25. Additional storage may be provided outside of the dimensions required by 4.25.

(5) All controls in accessible units, sleeping rooms, and suites shall comply with 4.27.

(6) Where provided as part of an accessible unit, sleeping room, or suite, the following spaces shall be accessible and shall be on an accessible route:

(a) the living area.

(b) the dining area.

(c) at least one sleeping area.

(d) patios, terraces, or balconies.

EXCEPTION: The requirements of 4.13.8 and 4.3.8 do not apply where it is necessary to utilize a higher door threshold or a change in level to protect the integrity of the unit from wind/water damage. Where this exception results in patios, terraces or balconies that are not at an accessible level, equivalent facilitation shall be provided. (e.g., Equivalent facilitation at a hotel patio or balcony might consist of providing raised decking or a ramp to provide accessibility).

(e) at least one full bathroom (i.e., one with a water closet, a lavatory, and a bathtub or shower).

(f) if only half baths are provided, at least one half bath.

(g) carports, garages or parking spaces.

(7) Kitchens, Kitchenettes, or Wet Bars. When provided as accessory to a sleeping room or suite, kitchens, kitchenettes, wet bars, or similar amenities shall be accessible. Clear floor space for a front or parallel approach to cabinets, counters, sinks, and appliances shall be provided to comply with 4.2.4.

Countertops and sinks shall be mounted at a maximum height of 34 in (865 mm) above the floor. At least fifty percent of shelf space in cabinets or refrigerator/freezers shall be within the reach ranges of 4.2.5 or 4.2.6 and space shall be designed to allow for the operation of cabinet and/or appliance doors so that all cabinets and appliances are accessible and usable. Controls and operating mechanisms shall comply with 4.27.

(8) Sleeping room accommodations for persons with hearing impairments required by 9.1 and complying with 9.3 shall be provided in the accessible sleeping room or suite.

9.3 Visual Alarms, Notification Devices and Telephones.

9.3.1 General. In sleeping rooms required to comply with this section, auxiliary visual alarms shall be provided and shall comply with 4.28.4. Visual notification devices shall also be provided in units, sleeping rooms and suites to alert room occupants of incoming telephone calls and a door knock or bell. Notification devices shall not be connected to auxiliary visual alarm signal appliances. Permanently installed telephones shall have volume controls complying with 4.31.5; an accessible electrical outlet within 4 ft (1220 mm) of a telephone connection shall be provided to facilitate the use of a text telephone.

9.3.2 Equivalent Facilitation. For purposes of this section, equivalent facilitation shall include the installation of electrical outlets (including outlets connected to a facility's central alarm system) and telephone wiring in sleeping rooms and suites to enable persons with hearing impairments to utilize portable visual alarms and communication devices provided by the operator of the facility.

9.4 Other Sleeping Rooms and Suites. Doors and doorways designed to allow passage into and within all sleeping units or other covered units shall comply with 4.13.5.

9.5 Transient Lodging in Homeless Shelters, Halfway Houses, Transient Group Homes, and Other Social Service Establishments.

9.5.1 New Construction. In new construction all public use and common use areas are required to be designed and constructed to comply with section 4. At least one of each type of amenity (such as washers, dryers and similar equipment installed for the use of occupants) in each common area shall be accessible and shall be located on an accessible route to any accessible unit or sleeping accommodation.

EXCEPTION: Where elevators are not provided as allowed in 4.1.3(5), accessible amenities are not required on inaccessible floors as long as one of each type is provided in common areas on accessible floors.

9.5.2 Alterations.

(1) Social service establishments which are not homeless shelters:

(a) The provisions of 9.5.3 and 9.1.5 shall apply to sleeping rooms and beds.

(b) Alteration of other areas shall be consistent with the new construction provisions of 9.5.1.

(2) Homeless shelters. If the following elements are altered, the following requirements apply:

(a) at least one public entrance shall allow a person with mobility impairments to approach, enter and exit including a minimum clear door width of 32 in (815 mm).

(b) sleeping space for homeless persons as provided in the scoping provisions of 9.1.2 shall include doors to the sleeping area with a minimum clear width of 32 in (815 mm) and maneuvering space around the beds for persons with mobility impairments complying with 9.2.2(1).

(c) at least one toilet room for each gender or one unisex toilet room shall have a minimum clear door width of 32 in (815 mm), minimum turning space complying with 4.2.3, one water closet complying with 4.16, one lavatory complying with 4.19 and the door shall have a privacy latch; and, if provided, at least one tub or shower shall comply with 4.20 or 4.21, respectively.

(d) at least one common area which a person with mobility impairments can approach, enter and exit including a minimum clear door width of 32 in (815 mm).

(e) at least one route connecting elements (a), (b), (c) and (d) which a person with mobility impairments can use including minimum clear width of 36 in (915 mm), passing space complying with 4.3.4, turning space complying with 4.2.3 and changes in levels complying with 4.3.8.

(f) homeless shelters can comply with the provisions of (a)-(e) by providing the above elements on one accessible floor.

9.5.3. Accessible Sleeping Accommodations in New Construction. Accessible sleeping rooms shall be provided in conformance with the table in 9.1.2 and shall comply with 9.2 Accessible Units, Sleeping Rooms and Suites (where the items are provided). Additional sleeping rooms that comply with 9.3 Sleeping Accommodations for Persons with Hearing Impairments shall be provided in conformance with the table provided in 9.1.3.

In facilities with multi-bed rooms or spaces, a percentage of the beds equal to the table provided in 9.1.2 shall comply with 9.2.2(1).

10. TRANSPORTATION FACILITIES.

10.1 General. Every station, bus stop, bus stop pad, terminal, building or other transportation facility, shall comply with the applicable provisions of 4.1 through 4.35, sections 5 through 9, and the applicable provisions of this section. The exceptions for elevators in 4.1.3(5), exception 1 and 4.1.6(l)(k) do not apply to a terminal, depot, or other station used for specified public transportation, or an airport passenger terminal, or facilities subject to Title II.

10.2 Bus Stops and Terminals.

10.2.1 New Construction

(1) Where new bus stop pads are constructed at bus stops, bays or other areas where a lift or ramp is to be deployed, they shall have a firm, stable surface; a minimum clear length of 96 inches (measured from the curb or vehicle roadway edge) and a minimum clear width of 60 inches (measured parallel to the vehicle roadway) to the maximum extent allowed by legal or site constraints; and shall be connected to streets, sidewalks or pedestrian paths by an accessible route complying with 4.3 and 4.4. The slope of the pad parallel to the roadway shall, to the extent practicable, be same as the roadway. For water drainage, a maximum slope of 1:50 (2%) perpendicular to the roadway is allowed.

(2) Where provided, new or replaced bus shelters shall be installed or positioned so as to permit a wheelchair or mobility aid user to enter from the public way and to reach a location, having a minimum clear floor area of 30 inches by 48 inches, entirely within the perimeter of the shelter. Such shelters shall be connected by an accessible route to the boarding area provided under paragraph (1) of this section.

(3) Where provided, all new bus route identification signs shall comply with 4.30.5. In addition, to the maximum extent practicable, all new bus route identification signs shall comply with 4.30.2 and 4.30.3. Signs that are sized to the maximum dimensions permitted under legitimate local, state or federal regulations or ordinances shall be considered in compliance with 4.30.2 and 4.30.3 for purposes of this section.

EXCEPTION: Bus schedules, timetables, or maps that are posted at the bus stop or bus bay are not required to comply with this provision.

10.2.2 Bus Stop Siting and Alterations.

(1) Bus stop sites shall be chosen such that, to the maximum extent practicable, the areas where lifts or ramps are to be deployed comply with 10.2.1(1) and (2)

(2) When new bus route identification signs are installed or old signs replaced, they shall comply with the requirements 10.2.1(3).

10.3 Fixed Facilities and Stations.

10.3.1 New Construction

New stations in rapid rail, light rail, commuter rail, intercity bus, intercity rail, high speed rail, and other fixed guideway systems (e.g., automated guideway transit, monorails, etc.) shall comply with the following provisions, as applicable:

(1) Elements such as ramps, elevators or other circulation devices, fare vending or other ticketing areas, and fare collection areas shall be placed to minimize the distance which wheelchair users and other persons who cannot negotiate steps have to travel compared to the general public. The circulation path, including an accessible entrance and accessible route, for

persons with disabilities shall, to the maximum extent practicable, coincide with the circulation path for the general public. Where the circulation path is different, signage complying with 4.30.1, 4.30.2, 4.30.3, 4.30.5, and 4.30.7(1) shall be provided to indicate direction to and identify the accessible entrance and accessible route.

(2) In lieu of compliance with 4.1.3(8), at least one entrance to each station shall comply with 4.14, Entrances. If different entrances to a station serve different transportation fixed routes or groups of fixed routes, at least one entrance serving each group or route shall comply with 4.14, Entrances. All accessible entrances shall, to the maximum extent practicable, coincide with those used by the majority of the general public.

(3) Direct connections to commercial, retail, or residential facilities shall have an accessible route complying with 4.3 from the point of connection to boarding platforms and all transportation system elements used by the public. Any elements provided to facilitate future direct connections shall be on an accessible route connecting boarding platforms and all transportation system elements used by the public.

(4) Where signs are provided at entrances to stations identifying the station or the entrance, or both, at least one sign at each entrance shall comply with 4.30.4 and 4.30.6. Such signs shall be placed in uniform locations at entrances within the transit system to the maximum extent practicable.

EXCEPTION: Where the station has no defined entrance, but signage is provided, then the accessible signage shall be placed in a central location.

(5) Stations covered by this section shall have identification signs complying with 4.30.1, 4.30.2, 4.30.3, and 4.30.5. Signs shall be placed at frequent intervals and shall be clearly visible from within the vehicle on both sides when not obstructed by another train. When station identification signs are placed close to vehicle windows (i.e., on side opposite from boarding) each shall have top of the highest letter or symbol below the top of the vehicle window and the bottom of the lowest letter or symbol above the horizontal mid-line of the vehicle window.

(6) Lists of stations, routes, or destinations served by the station and located on boarding areas, platforms, or mezzanines shall comply with 4.30.1, 4.30.2, 4.30.3, and 4.30.5. A minimum of one sign identifying the specific station and complying with 4.30.4 and 4.30.6 shall be provided on each platform or boarding area. All signs referenced in this paragraph shall, to the maximum extent practicable, be placed in uniform locations within the transit system.

(7)* Automatic fare vending, collection and adjustment (e.g. add-fare) systems shall comply with 4.34.2, 4.34.3, 4.34.4, and 4.34.5. At each accessible entrance such devices shall be located on an accessible route. If self-service fare collection devices are provided for the use of the general public, at least one accessible device for entering, and at least one for exiting, unless one device serves both functions, shall be provided at each accessible point of entry or exit. Accessible fare collection devices shall have a minimum clear opening width of 32 inches; shall permit passage of a wheelchair; and where provided, coin or card slots and controls necessary for operation shall comply with 4.27. Gates which must be pushed open by wheelchair or mobility aid users shall have a smooth continuous surface extending from 2 inches above the floor to 27 inches above the floor and shall comply with 4.13. Where the circulation path does not coincide with that used by the general public, accessible fare collection systems shall be located at or adjacent to the accessible point of entry or exit.

(8) Platform edges bordering a drop-off and not protected by platform screens or guard rails shall have a detectable warning. Such detectable warnings shall comply with 4.29.2 and shall be 24 inches wide running the full length of the platform drop-off.

(9) In stations covered by this section, rail-to-platform height in new stations shall be coordinated with the floor height of new vehicles so that the vertical difference, measured when the vehicle is at rest, is within plus or minus 5/8 inch under normal passenger load conditions. For rapid rail, light rail, commuter rail, high speed rail, and intercity rail systems in new stations, the horizontal gap, measured when the new vehicle is at rest, shall be no greater than 3 inches. For slow moving automated guideway "people mover" transit systems, the horizontal gap in new stations shall be no greater than I inch.

EXCEPTION 1: Existing vehicles operating in new stations may have a vertical difference with respect to the new platform within plus or minus 1-1/2 inches.

EXCEPTION 2: In light rail, commuter rail and intercity rail systems where it is not operationally or structurally feasible to meet the horizontal gap or vertical difference requirements, mini-high platforms, car-borne or platform-mounted lifts, ramps or bridge plates, or similar manually deployed devices, meeting the applicable requirements of 36 CFR part 1192, or 49 CFR part 38 shall suffice.

(10) Stations shall not be designed or constructed so as to require persons with disabilities to board or alight from a vehicle at a location other than one used by the general public.

(11) Illumination levels in the areas where signage is located shall be uniform and shall minimize glare on signs. Lighting along circulation routes shall be of a type and configuration to provide uniform illumination.

(12) Text Telephones: The following shall be provided in accordance with 4.31.9:

(a) If an interior public pay telephone is provided in a transit facility (as defined by the Department of Transportation), at least one interior public text telephone shall be provided in the station.

(b) Where four or more public pay telephones serve a particular entrance to a rail station and at least one is an interior location, at least one interior public text telephone shall be provided to serve that entrance. Compliance with this section constitutes compliance with section 4.1.3(17)(c).

(13) Where it is necessary to cross tracks to reach boarding platforms, the route surface shall be level and flush with the rail

top at the outer edge and between the rails, except for a maximum 2-1/2 inch gap on the inner edge of each rail to permit passage of wheel flanges. Such crossings shall comply with 4.29.5. Where gap reduction is not practicable, an above-grade or below-grade accessible route shall be provided.

(14) Where public address system are provided to convey information to the public in terminals, stations, or other fixed facilities, a means of conveying the same or equivalent information to persons with hearing loss or who are deaf shall be provided.

(15) Where clocks are provided for use by the general public, the clock face shall be uncluttered so that its elements are clearly visible. Hands, numerals, and/or digits shall contrast with the background either light-on-dark or dark-on-light. Where clocks are mounted overhead, numerals and/or digits shall comply with 4.30.3. Clocks shall be placed in uniform locations throughout the facility and system to the maximum extent practicable.

(16) Where provided in below grade stations, escalators shall have a minimum clear width of 32 inches. At the top and bottom of each escalator run, at least two contiguous treads shall level beyond comb plate before risers begin to form. All escalator treads shall be marked by a strip of clearly contrasting color, 2 inches in width, placed parallel to and on the nose of each step. The strip shall be as slip resistant as the remainder of the tread. The edge of the tread shall be apparent from both ascending and descending directions.

(17) Where provided, elevators shall be glazed or have transparent panels to allow unobstructed view both in to and out of the car. Elevators shall comply with 4.10.

EXCEPTION: Elevator cars with a clear floor area in which a 60 inch diameter circle can be inscribed may be substituted for the minimum car dimensions of 4.10, Fig. 22.

(18) Where provided, ticketing areas shall permit persons with disabilities to obtain a ticket and check baggage and shall comply with 7.2.

(19) Where provided, baggage check-in and retrieval systems shall be on an accessible route complying with 4.3. and shall have space immediately adjacent complying with 4.2. If unattended security barriers are provided, at least one gate shall comply with 4.13. Gates which must be pushed open by wheelchair or mobility aid users shall have smooth continuous surface extending from 2 inches above the floor to 27 inches above the floor.

10.3.2 Existing Facilities: Key Stations.

(1) Rapid, light and commuter rail key stations, as defined under criteria established by the Department of Transportation in subpart C of 49 CFR part 37 and existing intercity rail stations shall provide at least one accessible route from an accessible entrance to those areas necessary for use of the transportation system.

(2) The accessible route required by 10.3.2(1) shall include features specified in 10.3.1(1), (4)-(9), (11)-(15), and (17)-(19).

(3) Where technical infeasibility in existing stations requires the accessible route to lead from the public way to a paid area of the transit system, an accessible fare collection system, complying with 10.3.1(7), shall be provided along such accessible route.

(4) In light rail, rapid rail and commuter rail key stations, the platform or a portion thereof and the vehicle floor shall be coordinated so that the vertical difference, measured when the vehicle is at rest, is within plus or minus 1- 1/2 inches under all normal passenger load conditions, and the horizontal gap, measured when the vehicle is at rest, is no greater than 3 inches for at least one door of each vehicle or car required to be accessible by 49 CFR part 37.

EXCEPTION 1: Existing vehicles retrofitted to meet the requirements of 49 CFR 37.93 (one-car-per-train rule) shall be coordinated with the platform such that, for at least one door, the vertical difference between the vertical floor and the platform, measured when the vehicle is at rest with 50% normal passenger capacity, is within plus or minus 2 inches and the horizontal gap is no greater than 4 inches.

EXCEPTION 2: Where it is not structurally or operationally feasible to meet the horizontal gap or vertical difference requirements, mini-high platforms, car-borne or platform mounted lifts, ramps or bridge plates, or similar manually deployed devices, meeting the applicable requirements of 36 CFR part 1192 or 49 CFR part 38, shall suffice.

(5) New direct connections to commercial, retail, or residential facilities shall, to the maximum extent feasible, have an accessible route complying with 4.3 from the point of connection to boarding platforms and all transportation system elements used by the public. Any elements provided to facilitate future direct connections shall be on an accessible route connecting boarding platforms and all transportation system elements used by the public.

10.3.3 Existing Facilities: Alterations.

(1) For the purpose of complying with 4.1.6(2) Alterations to an Area Containing a Primary Function, an area of primary function shall be as defined by applicable provisions of 49 CFR 37.43(c) (Department of Transportation's ADA Rule) or 28 CFR 36.403 (Department of Justice's ADA Rule).

10.4 Airports.

10.4.1 New Construction.

(1) Elements such as ramps, elevators or other vertical circulation devices, ticketing areas, security checkpoints, or passenger waiting areas shall be placed to minimize the distance which wheelchair users and other persons who cannot negotiate steps may have to travel compared to the general public.

(2) The circulation path, including an accessible entrance and an accessible route, for persons with disabilities shall, to the

maximum extent practicable, coincide with the circulation path for the general public. Where the circulation path is different, directional signage complying with 4.30.1, 4.30.2, 4.30.3 and 4.30.5 shall be provided which indicates the location of the nearest accessible entrance and its accessible route.

(3) Ticketing areas shall permit persons with disabilities to obtain a ticket and check baggage and shall comply with 7.2.

(4) Where public pay telephones are provided, and at least one is at an interior location, a public text telephone shall be provided in compliance with 4.31.9. Additionally, if four or more public pay telephones are located in any of the following locations, at least one public text telephone shall also be provided in that location:

> (a) a main terminal outside the security areas;
>
> (b) a concourse within the security areas; or
>
> (c) a baggage claim area in a terminal.

Compliance with this section constitutes compliance with section 4.1.3(17)(c).

(5) Baggage check-in and retrieval systems shall be on an accessible route complying with 4.3, and shall have space immediately adjacent complying with 4.2.4. If unattended security barriers are provided, at least one shall comply with 4.13. Gates which must be pushed open by wheelchair or mobility aid users shall have a smooth continuous surface extending from 2 inches above the floor to 27 inches above the floor.

(6) Terminal Information systems which broadcast information to the general public through a public address system shall provide a means to provide the same or equivalent information to persons with hearing loss or who are deaf. Such methods may include, but are not limited to, visual paging systems using video monitors and computer technology. For persons with certain types of hearing loss such methods may include, but are not limited to an assistive listening system complying with 4.33.7.

(7) Where clocks are provided for use by the general public the clock face shall be uncluttered so that elements are clearly visible. Hands, numerals, and/or digits shall contrast with their background either light-on-dark or dark-on-light. Where clocks are mounted overhead, numerals and/or digits shall comply with 4.30.3. Clocks shall be placed in uniform locations throughout the facility to the maximum extent practicable.

(8) Security Systems. [Reserved]

10.5 Boat and Ferry Docks.
[Reserved]

APPENDIX

This appendix contains materials of an advisory nature and provides additional information that should help the reader to understand the minimum requirements of the guidelines or to design buildings or facilities for greater accessibility. The paragraph numbers correspond to the sections or paragraphs of the guideline to which the material relates and are therefore not consecutive (for example, A4.2.1 contains additional information relevant to 4.2.1). Sections of the guidelines for which additional material appears in this appendix have been indicated by an asterisk. Nothing in this appendix shall in any way obviate any obligation to comply with the requirements of the guidelines itself.

A2.2 Equivalent Facilitation. Specific examples of equivalent facilitation are found in the following sections:

4.1.6(3)(c)	Elevators in Alterations
4.31.9	Text Telephones
7.2	Sales and Service Counters, Teller Windows, Information Counters
9.1.4	Classes of Sleeping Accommodations
9.2.2(6)(d)	Requirements for Accessible Units, Sleeping Rooms, and Suites

A4.1.1 Application.

A4.1.1(3) Areas Used Only by Employees as Work Areas. Where there are a series of individual work stations of the same type (e.g., laboratories, service counters, ticket booths), 5%, but not less than one, of each type of work station should be constructed so that an individual with disabilities can maneuver within the work stations. Rooms housing individual offices in a typical office building must meet the requirements of the guidelines concerning doors, accessible routes, etc. but do not need to allow for maneuvering space around individual desks. Modifications required to permit maneuvering within the work area may be accomplished as a reasonable accommodation to individual employees with disabilities under Title I of the ADA. Consideration should also be given to placing shelves in employee work areas at a convenient height for accessibility or installing commercially available shelving that is adjustable so that reasonable accommodations can be made in the future.

If work stations are made accessible they should comply with the applicable provisions of 4.2 through 4.35.

A4.1.2 Accessible Sites and Exterior Facilities: New Construction.

A4.1.2(5)(e) Valet Parking. Valet parking is not always usable by individuals with disabilities. For instance, an individual may use a type of vehicle controls that render the regular controls inoperable or the driver's seat in a van may be removed. In these situations, another person cannot park the vehicle. It is recommended that some self-parking spaces be provided at valet parking facilities for individuals whose vehicles cannot be parked by another person and that such spaces be located on an accessible route to the entrance of the facility.

A4.1.3 Accessible Buildings: New Construction.

A4.1.3(5) Only full passenger elevators are covered by the accessibility provisions of 4.10. Materials and equipment hoists, freight elevators not intended for passenger use, dumbwaiters, and construction elevators are not covered by these guidelines. If a building is exempt from the elevator requirement, it is not necessary to provide a platform lift or other means of vertical access in lieu of an elevator.

Under Exception 4, platform lifts are allowed where existing conditions make it impractical to install a ramp or elevator. Such conditions generally occur where it is essential to provide access to small raised or lowered areas where space may not be available for a ramp. Examples include, but are not limited to, raised pharmacy platforms, commercial offices raised above a sales floor, or radio and news booths.

A4.1.3(9) Supervised automatic sprinkler systems have built in signals for monitoring features of the system such as the opening and closing of water control valves, the power supplies for needed pumps, water tank levels, and for indicating conditions that will impair the satisfactory operation of the sprinkler system. Because of these monitoring features, supervised automatic sprinkler systems have a high level of satisfactory performance and response to fire conditions.

A4.1.3(10) If an odd number of drinking fountains is provided on a floor, the requirement in 4.1.3(10)(b) may be met by rounding down the odd number to an even number and calculating 50% of the even number. When more than one drinking fountain on a floor is required to comply with 4.15, those fountains should be dispersed to allow wheelchair users convenient access. For example, in a large facility such as a convention center that has water fountains at several locations on a floor, the accessible water fountains should be located so that wheelchair users do not have to travel a greater distance than other people to use a drinking fountain.

A4.1.3(17)(b) In addition to the requirements of section 4.1.3(17)(b), the installation of additional volume controls is encouraged. Volume controls may be installed on any telephone.

A4.1.3(19)(a) Readily removable or folding seating units may be installed in lieu of providing an open space for wheelchair users. Folding seating units are usually two fixed seats that can be easily folded into a fixed center bar to allow for one or two open spaces for wheelchair users when necessary. These units are more easily adapted than removable seats which generally require the seat to be removed in advance by the facility management.

Either a sign or a marker placed on seating with removable or folding arm rests is required by this section. Consideration should be given for ensuring identification of such seats in a darkened theater. For example, a marker which contrasts (light on dark or dark on light) and which also reflects light could be placed on the side of such seating so as to be visible in a lighted auditorium and also to reflect light from a flashlight.

A4.1.6 Accessible Buildings: Alterations.

A4.1.6(1)(h) When an entrance is being altered, it is preferable that those entrances being altered be made accessible to the extent feasible.

A4.2 Space Allowances and Reach Ranges.

A4.2.1 Wheelchair Passage Width.

(1) Space Requirements for Wheelchairs. Many persons who use wheelchairs need a 30 in (760 mm) clear opening width for doorways, gates, and the like, when the latter are entered head-on. If the person is unfamiliar with a building, if competing traffic is heavy, if sudden or frequent movements are needed, or if the wheelchair must be turned at an opening, then greater clear widths are needed. For most situations, the addition of an inch of leeway on either side is sufficient. Thus, a minimum clear width of 32 in (815 mm) will provide adequate clearance. However, when an opening or a restriction in a passageway is more than 24 in (610 mm) long, it is essentially a passageway and must be at least 36 in (915 mm) wide.

(2) Space Requirements for Use of Walking Aids. Although people who use walking aids can maneuver through clear width openings of 32 in (815 mm), they need 36 in (915 mm) wide passageways and walks for comfortable gaits. Crutch tips, often extending down at a wide angle, are a hazard in narrow passageways where they might not be seen by other pedestrians. Thus, the 36 in (915 mm) width provides a safety allowance both for the person with a disability and for others.

(3) Space Requirements for Passing. Able-bodied persons in winter clothing, walking straight ahead with arms swinging, need 32 in (815 mm) of width, which includes 2 in (50 mm) on either side for sway, and another 1 in (25 mm) tolerance on either side for clearing nearby objects or other pedestrians. Almost all wheelchair users and those who use walking aids can also manage within this 32 in (815 mm) width for short distances. Thus, two streams of traffic can pass in 64 in (1625 mm) in a comfortable flow. Sixty inches (1525 mm) provides a minimum width for a somewhat more restricted flow. If the clear width is less than 60 in (1525 mm), two wheelchair users will not be able to pass but will have to seek a wider place for passing. Forty-eight inches (1220 mm) is the minimum width needed for an ambulatory person to pass a nonambulatory or semi-ambulatory person. Within this 48 in (1220 mm) width, the ambulatory person will have to twist to pass a wheelchair user, a person with a service animal, or a semi-ambulatory person. There will be little leeway for swaying or missteps (see Fig. A1).

A4.2.3 Wheelchair Turning Space. These guidelines specify a minimum space of 60 in (1525 mm) diameter or a 60 in by 60 in (1525 mm by 1525 mm) T-shaped space for a pivoting 180-degree turn of a wheelchair. This space is usually satisfactory for turning around, but many people will not be able to turn without repeated tries and bumping into surrounding objects. The space shown in Fig. A2 will allow most wheelchair users to complete U-turns without difficulty.

A4.2.4 Clear Floor or Ground Space for Wheelchairs. The wheelchair and user shown in Fig. A3 represent typical dimensions for a large adult male. The space requirements in this guideline are based upon maneuvering clearances that will accommodate most wheelchairs. Fig. A3 provides a uniform reference for design not covered by this guideline.

A4.2.5 & A4.2.6 Reach. Reach ranges for persons seated in wheelchairs may be further clarified by Fig. A3(a). These drawings approximate in the plan view the information shown in Fig. 4, 5, and 6.

A4.3 Accessible Route.

A4.3.1 General.

(1) Travel Distances. Many people with mobility impairments can move at only very slow speeds; for many, traveling 200 ft (61 m) could take about 2 minutes. This assumes a rate of about 1.5 ft/s (455 mm/s) on level ground. It also assumes that the traveler would move continuously. However, on trips over 100 ft (30 m), disabled people are apt to rest frequently, which substantially increases their trip times. Resting periods of 2 minutes for every 100 ft (30 m) can be used to estimate travel times for people with severely limited stamina. In inclement weather, slow progress and resting can greatly increase a disabled person's exposure to the elements.

(2) Sites. Level, indirect routes or those with running slopes lower than 1:20 can sometimes provide more convenience than direct routes with maximum allowable slopes or with ramps.

A4.3.10 Egress. Because people with disabilities may visit, be employed or be a resident in any building, emergency management plans with specific provisions to ensure their safe evacuation also play an essential role in fire safety and life safety.

A4.3.11.3 Stairway Width. A 48 in (1220 mm) wide exit stairway is needed to allow assisted evacuation (e.g., carrying a person in a wheelchair) without encroaching on the exit path for ambulatory persons.

A4.3.11.4 Two-way Communication. It is essential that emergency communication not be dependent on voice communications alone because the safety of people with hearing or speech impairments could be jeopardized. The visible signal requirement could be satisfied with something as simple as a button in the area of rescue assistance that lights, indicating that help is on the way, when the message is answered at the point of entry.

A4.4 Protruding Objects.

A4.4.1 General. Service animals are trained to recognize and avoid hazards. However, most people with severe impairments of vision use the long cane as an aid to mobility. The two principal cane techniques are the touch technique, where the cane arcs from side to side and touches points outside both shoulders; and the diagonal technique, where the cane is held in a stationary position diagonally across the body with the cane tip touching or just above the ground at a point outside one shoulder and the handle or grip extending to a point outside the other shoulder. The touch technique is used primarily in uncontrolled areas, while the diagonal technique is used primarily in certain limited, controlled, and familiar environments. Cane users are often trained to use both techniques.

Potential hazardous objects are noticed only if they fall within the detection range of canes (see Fig. A4). Visually impaired people walking toward an object can detect an overhang if its lowest surface is not higher than 27 in (685 mm). When walking alongside protruding objects, they cannot detect overhangs. Since proper cane and service animal techniques keep people away from the edge of a path or from walls, a slight overhang of no more than 4 in (100 mm) is not hazardous.

A4.5 Ground and Floor Surfaces.

A4.5.1 General. People who have difficulty walking or maintaining balance or who use crutches, canes, or walkers, and those with restricted gaits are particularly sensitive to slipping and tripping hazards. For such people, a stable and regular surface is necessary for safe walking, particularly on stairs. Wheelchairs can be propelled most easily on surfaces that are hard, stable, and regular. Soft loose surfaces such as shag carpet, loose sand or gravel, wet clay, and irregular surfaces such as cobblestones can significantly impede wheelchair movement.

Slip resistance is based on the frictional force necessary to keep a shoe heel or crutch tip from slipping on a walking surface under conditions likely to be found on the surface. While the dynamic coefficient of friction during walking varies in a complex and non-uniform way, the static coefficient of friction, which can be measured in several ways, provides a close approximation of the slip resistance of a surface. Contrary to popular belief, some slippage is necessary to walking, especially for persons with restricted gaits; a truly "non-slip" surface could not be negotiated.

The Occupational Safety and Health Administration recommends that walking surfaces have a static coefficient of friction of 0.5. A research project sponsored by the Architectural and Transportation Barriers Compliance Board (Access Board) conducted tests with persons with disabilities and concluded that a higher coefficient of friction was needed by such persons. A static coefficient of friction of 0.6 is recommended for accessible routes and 0.8 for ramps.

It is recognized that the coefficient of friction varies considerably due to the presence of contaminants, water, floor finishes, and other factors not under the control of the designer or builder and not subject to design and construction guidelines and that compliance would be difficult to measure on the building site. Nevertheless, many common building materials suitable for flooring are now labeled with information on the static coefficient of friction. While it may not be possible to compare one product directly with another, or to guarantee a constant measure, builders and designers are encouraged to specify materials with appropriate values. As more products include information on slip resistance, improved uniformity in measurement and specification is likely. The Access Board's advisory guidelines on Slip

Resistant Surfaces provides additional information on this subject.

Cross slopes on walks and ground or floor surfaces can cause considerable difficulty in propelling a wheelchair in a straight line.

A4.5.3 Carpet. Much more needs to be done in developing both quantitative and qualitative criteria for carpeting (i.e., problems associated with texture and weave need to be studied). However, certain functional characteristics are well established. When both carpet and padding are used, it is desirable to have minimum movement (preferably none) between the floor and the pad and the pad and the carpet which would allow the carpet to hump or warp. In heavily trafficked areas, a thick, soft (plush) pad or cushion, particularly in combination with long carpet pile, makes it difficult for individuals in wheelchairs and those with other ambulatory disabilities to get about. Firm carpeting can be achieved through proper selection and combination of pad and carpet, sometimes with the elimination of the pad or cushion, and with proper installation. Carpeting designed with a weave that causes a zigzag effect when wheeled across is strongly discouraged.

A4.6 Parking and Passenger Loading Zones.

A4.6.3 Parking Spaces. The increasing use of vans with side-mounted lifts or ramps by persons with disabilities has necessitated some revisions in specifications for parking spaces and adjacent access aisles. The typical accessible parking space is 96 in (2440 mm) wide with an adjacent 60 in (1525 mm) access aisle. However, this aisle does not permit lifts or ramps to be deployed and still leave room for a person using a wheelchair or other mobility aid to exit the lift platform or ramp. In tests conducted with actual lift/van/wheelchair combinations, (under a Board-sponsored Accessible Parking and Loading Zones Project) researchers found that a space and aisle totalling almost 204 in (5180 mm) wide was needed to deploy a lift and exit conveniently. The "van accessible" parking space required by these guidelines provides a 96 in (2440 mm) wide space with a 96 in (2440 mm) adjacent access aisle which is just wide enough to maneuver and exit from a side mounted lift. If a 96 in (2440 mm) access aisle is placed between two spaces, two "van accessible" spaces are created. Alternatively, if the wide access aisle is provided at the end of a row (an area often unused), it may be possible to provide the wide access aisle without additional space (see Fig. A5(a)).

A sign is needed to alert van users to the presence of the wider aisle, but the space is not intended to be restricted only to vans.

"Universal" Parking Space Design. An alternative to the provision of a percentage of spaces with a wide aisle, and the associated need to include additional signage, is the use of what has been called the "universal" parking space design. Under this design, all accessible spaces are 132 in (3350 mm) wide with a 60 in (1525 mm) access aisle (see Fig. A5(b)). One advantage to this design is that no additional signage is needed because all spaces can accommodate a van with a side-mounted lift or ramp. Also, there is no competition between cars and vans for spaces since all spaces can accommodate either. Furthermore, the wider space permits vehicles to park to one side or the other within the 132 in (3350 mm) space to allow persons to exit and enter the vehicle on either the driver or passenger side, although, in some cases, this would require exiting or entering without a marked access aisle.

An essential consideration for any design is having the access aisle level with the parking space. Since a person with a disability, using a lift or ramp, must maneuver within the access aisle, the aisle cannot include a ramp or sloped area. The access aisle must be connected to an accessible route to the appropriate accessible entrance of a building or facility. The parking access aisle must either blend with the accessible route or have a curb ramp complying with 4.7. Such a curb ramp opening must be located within the access aisle boundaries, not within the parking space boundaries. Unfortunately, many facilities are designed with a ramp that is blocked when any vehicle parks in the accessible space. Also, the required dimensions of the access aisle cannot be restricted by planters, curbs or wheel stops.

A4.6.4 Signage. Signs designating parking places for disabled people can be seen from a driver's seat if the signs are mounted high enough above the ground and located at the front of a parking space.

A4.6.5 Vertical Clearance. High-top vans, which disabled people or transportation services often use, require higher clearances in parking garages than automobiles.

A4.8 Ramps.

A4.8.1 General. Ramps are essential for wheelchair users if elevators or lifts are not available to connect different levels. However, some people who use walking aids have difficulty with ramps and prefer stairs.

A4.8.2 Slope and Rise. Ramp slopes between 1:16 and 1:20 are preferred. The ability to manage an incline is related to both its slope and its length. Wheelchair users with disabilities affecting their arms or with low stamina have serious difficulty using inclines. Most ambulatory people and most people who use wheelchairs can manage a slope of 1:16. Many people cannot manage a slope of 1:12 for 30 ft (9 m).

A4.8.4 Landings. Level landings are essential toward maintaining an aggregate slope that complies with these guidelines. A ramp landing that is not level causes individuals using wheelchairs to tip backward or bottom out when the ramp is approached.

A4.8.5 Handrails. The requirements for stair and ramp handrails in this guideline are for adults. When children are principal users in a building or facility, a second set of handrails at an appropriate height can assist them and aid in preventing accidents.

A4.9 Stairs.

A4.9.1 Minimum Number. Only interior and exterior stairs connecting levels that are not connected by an elevator, ramp, or other accessible means of vertical access have to comply with

4.9.

A4.10 Elevators.

A4.10.6 Door Protective and Reopening Device. The required door reopening device would hold the door open for 20 seconds if the doorway remains obstructed. After 20 seconds, the door may begin to close. However, if designed in accordance with ASME A17.1-1990, the door closing movement could still be stopped if a person or object exerts sufficient force at any point on the door edge.

A4.10.7 Door and Signal Timing for Hall Calls. This paragraph allows variation in the location of call buttons, advance time for warning signals, and the door-holding period used to meet the time requirement.

A4.10.12 Car Controls. Industry-wide standardization of elevator control panel design would make all elevators significantly more convenient for use by people with severe visual impairments. In many cases, it will be possible to locate the highest control on elevator panels within 48 in (1220 mm) from the floor.

A4.10.13 Car Position Indicators. A special button may be provided that would activate the audible signal within the given elevator only for the desired trip, rather than maintaining the audible signal in constant operation.

A4.10.14 Emergency Communications. A device that requires no handset is easier to use by people who have difficulty reaching. Also, small handles on handset compartment doors are not usable by people who have difficulty grasping.

Ideally, emergency two-way communication systems should provide both voice and visual display intercommunication so that persons with hearing impairments and persons with vision impairments can receive information regarding the status of a rescue. A voice intercommunication system cannot be the only means of communication because it is not accessible to people with speech and hearing impairments. While a voice intercommunication system is not required, at a minimum, the system should provide both an audio and visual indication that a rescue is on the way.

A4.11 Platform Lifts (Wheelchair Lifts).

A4.11.2 Other Requirements. Inclined stairway chairlifts, and inclined and vertical platform lifts (wheelchair lifts) are available for short-distance, vertical transportation of people with disabilities. Care should be taken in selecting lifts as some lifts are not equally suitable for use by both wheelchair users and semi-ambulatory individuals.

A4.12 Windows.

A4.12.1 General. Windows intended to be operated by occupants in accessible spaces should comply with 4.12.

A4.12.2 Window Hardware. Windows requiring pushing, pulling, or lifting to open (for example, double-hung, sliding, or casement and awning units without cranks) should require no more than 5 lbf (22.2 N) to open or close. Locks, cranks, and other window hardware should comply with 4.27.

A4.13 Doors.

A4.13.8 Thresholds at Doorways. Thresholds and surface height changes in doorways are particularly inconvenient for wheelchair users who also have low stamina or restrictions in arm movement because complex maneuvering is required to get over the level change while operating the door.

A4.13.9 Door Hardware. Some disabled persons must push against a door with their chair or walker to open it. Applied kickplates on doors with closers can reduce required maintenance by withstanding abuse from wheelchairs and canes. To be effective, they should cover the door width, less approximately 2 in (51 mm), up to a height of 16 in (405 mm) from its bottom edge and be centered across the width of the door.

A4.13.10 Door Closers. Closers with delayed action features give a person more time to maneuver through doorways. They are particularly useful on frequently used interior doors such as entrances to toilet rooms.

A4.13.11 Door Opening Force. Although most people with disabilities can exert at least 5 lbf (22.2N), both pushing and pulling from a stationary position, a few people with severe disabilities cannot exert 3 lbf (13.13N). Although some people cannot manage the allowable forces in this guideline and many others have difficulty, door closers must have certain minimum closing forces to close doors satisfactorily. Forces for pushing or pulling doors open are measured with a push-pull scale under the following conditions:

(1) Hinged doors: Force applied perpendicular to the door at the door opener or 30 in (760 mm) from the hinged side, whichever is farther from the hinge.

(2) Sliding or folding doors: Force applied parallel to the door at the door pull or latch.

(3) Application of force: Apply force gradually so that the applied force does not exceed the resistance of the door. In high-rise buildings, air-pressure differentials may require a modification of this specification in order to meet the functional intent.

A4.13.12 Automatic Doors and Power-Assisted Doors. Sliding automatic doors do not need guard rails and are more convenient for wheelchair users and visually impaired people to use. If slowly opening automatic doors can be reactivated before their closing cycle is completed, they will be more convenient in busy doorways.

A4.15 Drinking Fountains and Water Coolers.

A4.15.2 Spout Height. Two drinking fountains, mounted side by side or on a single post, are usable by people with disabilities and people who find it difficult to bend over.

A4.16 Water Closets.

A4.16.3 Height. Height preferences for toilet seats vary considerably among disabled people. Higher seat heights may be an advantage to some ambulatory disabled people, but are often a disadvantage for wheelchair users and others. Toilet seats 18 in (455 mm) high seem to be a reasonable compromise. Thick seats and filler rings are available to adapt standard fixtures to these requirements.

A4.16.4 Grab Bars. Fig. A6(a) and (b) show the diagonal and side approaches most commonly used to transfer from a wheelchair to a water closet. Some wheelchair users can transfer from the front of the toilet while others use a 90-degree approach. Most people who use the two additional approaches can also use either the diagonal approach or the side approach.

A4.16.5 Flush Controls. Flush valves and related plumbing can be located behind walls or to the side of the toilet, or a toilet seat lid can be provided if plumbing fittings are directly behind the toilet seat. Such designs reduce the chance of injury and imbalance caused by leaning back against the fittings. Flush controls for tank-type toilets have a standardized mounting location on the left side of the tank (facing the tank). Tanks can be obtained by special order with controls mounted on the right side. If administrative authorities require flush controls for flush valves to be located in a position that conflicts with the location of the rear grab bar, then that bar may be split or shifted toward the wide side of the toilet area.

A4.17 Toilet Stalls.

A4.17.3 Size and Arrangement. This section requires use of the 60 in (1525 mm) standard stall (Figure 30(a)) and permits the 36 in (915 mm) or 48 in (1220 mm) wide alternate stall (Figure 30(b)) only in alterations where provision of the standard stall is technically infeasible or where local plumbing codes prohibit reduction in the number of fixtures. A standard stall provides a clear space on one side of the water closet to enable persons who use wheelchairs to perform a side or diagonal transfer from the wheelchair to the water closet. However, some persons with disabilities who use mobility aids such as walkers, canes or crutches are better able to use the two parallel grab bars in the 36 in (915 mm) wide alternate stall to achieve a standing position.

In large toilet rooms, where six or more toilet stalls are provided, it is therefore required that a 36 in (915 mm) wide stall with parallel grab bars be provided in addition to the standard stall required in new construction. The 36 in (915 mm) width is necessary to achieve proper use of the grab bars; wider stalls would position the grab bars too far apart to be easily used and narrower stalls would position the grab bars too close to the water closet. Since the stall is primarily intended for use by persons using canes, crutches and walkers, rather than wheelchairs, the length of the stall could be conventional. The door, however, must swing outward to ensure a usable space for people who use crutches or walkers.

A4.17.5 Doors. To make it easier for wheelchair users to close toilet stall doors, doors can be provided with closers, spring hinges, or a pull bar mounted on the inside surface of the door near the hinge side.

A4.19 Lavatories and Mirrors.

A4.19.6 Mirrors. If mirrors are to be used by both ambulatory people and wheelchair users, then they must be at least 74 in (1880 mm) high at their topmost edge. A single full length mirror can accommodate all people, including children.

A4.21 Shower Stalls.

A4.21.1 General. Shower stalls that are 36 in by 36 in (915 mm by 915 mm) wide provide additional safety to people who have difficulty maintaining balance because all grab bars and walls are within easy reach. Seated people use the walls of 36 in by 36 in (915 mm by 915 mm) showers for back support. Shower stalls that are 60 in (1525 mm) wide and have no curb may increase usability of a bathroom by wheelchair users because the shower area provides additional maneuvering space.

A4.22 Toilet Rooms.

A4.22.3 Clear Floor Space. In many small facilities, single-user restrooms may be the only facilities provided for all building users. In addition, the guidelines allow the use of "unisex" or "family" accessible toilet rooms in alterations when technical infeasibility can be demonstrated. Experience has shown that the provision of accessible "unisex" or single-user restrooms is a reasonable way to provide access for wheelchair users and any attendants, especially when attendants are of the opposite sex. Since these facilities have proven so useful, it is often considered advantageous to install a "unisex" toilet room in new facilities in addition to making the multi-stall restrooms accessible, especially in shopping malls, large auditoriums, and convention centers.

Figure 28 (section 4.16) provides minimum clear floor space dimensions for toilets in accessible "unisex" toilet rooms. The dotted lines designate the minimum clear floor space, depending on the direction of approach, required for wheelchair users to transfer onto the water closet. The dimensions of 48 in (1220 mm) and 60 in (1525 mm), respectively, correspond to the space required for the two common transfer approaches utilized by wheelchair users (see Fig. A6). It is important to keep in mind that the placement of the lavatory to the immediate side of the water closet will preclude the side approach transfer illustrated in Figure A6(b). To accommodate the side transfer, the space adjacent to the water closet must remain clear of obstruction for 42 in (1065 mm) from the centerline of the toilet (Figure 28) and the lavatory must not be located within this clear space. A turning circle or T-turn, the clear floor space at the lavatory, and maneuvering space at the door must be considered when determining the possible wall locations. A privacy latch or other accessible means of ensuring privacy during use should be provided at the door.

RECOMMENDATIONS:

1. In new construction, accessible single-user restrooms may be desirable in some situations because they can accommodate

a wide variety of building users. However, they cannot be used in lieu of making the multi-stall toilet rooms accessible as required.

2. Where strict compliance to the guidelines for accessible toilet facilities is technically infeasible in the alteration of existing facilities, accessible "unisex" toilets are a reasonable alternative.

3. In designing accessible single-user restrooms, the provisions of adequate space to allow a side transfer will provide accommodation to the largest number of wheelchair users.

A4.23 Bathrooms, Bathing Facilities, and Shower Rooms.

A4.23.3 Clear Floor Space. Figure A7 shows two possible configurations of a toilet room with a roll-in shower. The specific shower shown is designed to fit exactly within the dimensions of a standard bathtub. Since the shower does not have a lip, the floor space can be used for required maneuvering space. This would permit a toilet room to be smaller than would be permitted with a bathtub and still provide enough floor space to be considered accessible. This design can provide accessibility in facilities where space is at a premium (i.e., hotels and medical care facilities). The alternate roll-in shower (Fig. 57b) also provides sufficient room for the "T-turn" and does not require plumbing to be on more than one wall.

A4.23.9 Medicine Cabinets. Other alternatives for storing medical and personal care items are very useful to disabled people. Shelves, drawers, and floor-mounted cabinets can be provided within the reach ranges of disabled people.

A4.26 Handrails, Grab Bars, and Tub and Shower Seats.

A4.26.1 General. Many disabled people rely heavily upon grab bars and handrails to maintain balance and prevent serious falls. Many people brace their forearms between supports and walls to give them more leverage and stability in maintaining balance or for lifting. The grab bar clearance of 1-1/2 in (38 mm) required in this guideline is a safety clearance to prevent injuries resulting from arms slipping through the openings. It also provides adequate gripping room.

A4.26.2 Size and Spacing of Grab Bars and Handrails. This specification allows for alternate shapes of handrails as long as they allow an opposing grip similar to that provided by a circular section of 1-1/4 in to 1-1/2 in (32 mm to 38 mm).

A4.27 Controls and Operating Mechanisms.

A4.27.3 Height. Fig. A8 further illustrates mandatory and advisory control mounting height provisions for typical equipment.

Electrical receptacles installed to serve individual appliances and not intended for regular or frequent use by building occupants are not required to be mounted within the specified reach ranges. Examples would be receptacles installed specifically for wall-mounted clocks, refrigerators, and microwave ovens.

A4.28 Alarms.

A4.28.2 Audible Alarms. Audible emergency signals must have an intensity and frequency that can attract the attention of individuals who have partial hearing loss. People over 60 years of age generally have difficulty perceiving frequencies higher than 10,000 Hz. An alarm signal which has a periodic element to its signal, such as single stroke bells (clang-pause-clang-pause), hi-low (up-down-up-down) and fast whoop (on-off-on-off) are best. Avoid continuous or reverberating tones. Select a signal which has a sound characterized by three or four clear tones without a great deal of "noise" in between.

A4.28.3 Visual Alarms. The specifications in this section do not preclude the use of zoned or coded alarm systems.

A4.28.4 Auxiliary Alarms. Locating visual emergency alarms in rooms where persons who are deaf may work or reside alone can ensure that they will always be warned when an emergency alarm is activated. To be effective, such devices must be located and oriented so that they will spread signals and reflections throughout a space or raise the overall light level sharply. However, visual alarms alone are not necessarily the best means to alert sleepers. A study conducted by Underwriters Laboratory (UL) concluded that a flashing light more than seven times brighter was required (110 candela v. 15 candela, at the same distance) to awaken sleepers as was needed to alert awake subjects in a normal daytime illuminated room.

For hotel and other rooms where people are likely to be asleep, a signal-activated vibrator placed between mattress and box spring or under a pillow was found by UL to be much more effective in alerting sleepers. Many readily available devices are sound-activated so that they could respond to an alarm clock, clock radio, wake-up telephone call or room smoke detector. Activation by a building alarm system can either be accomplished by a separate circuit activating an auditory alarm which would, in turn, trigger the vibrator or by a signal transmitted through the ordinary 110-volt outlet. Transmission of signals through the power line is relatively simple and is the basis of common, inexpensive remote light control systems sold in many department and electronic stores for home use. So-called "wireless" intercoms operate on the same principal.

Requirements for detectable warnings at curb ramps, hazardous vehicular areas, and reflecting pools have been suspended until July 26, 1998. By that date, the ATBCB should issue a joint rule with the Departments of Justice and Transportation with respect to the need for and usability of current technical specifications for detectable warnings at curb ramps, hazardous vehicular areas, and reflecting pools.

A4.29.2 Detectable Warnings on Walking Surfaces. The material used to provide contrast should contrast by at least 70%. Contrast in percent is determined by:

$$\text{Contrast} = [(B1 - B2)/B1] \times 100$$

where B1 = light reflectance value (LRV) of the lighter area
and B2 = light reflectance value (LRV) of the darker area.

Note that in any application both white and black are never
absolute; thus, B1 never equals 100 and B2 is always greater
than 0.

A4.30 Signage.

A4.30.1 General. In building complexes where finding locations
independently on a routine basis may be a necessity (for
example, college campuses), tactile maps or prerecorded
instructions can be very helpful to visually impaired people.
Several maps and auditory instructions have been developed and
tested for specific applications. The type of map or instructions
used must be based on the information to be communicated,
which depends highly on the type of buildings or users.

Landmarks that can easily be distinguished by visually impaired
individuals are useful as orientation cues. Such cues include
changes in illumination level, bright colors, unique patterns, wall
murals, location of special equipment or other architectural
features.

Many people with disabilities have limitations in movement of their
heads and reduced peripheral vision. Thus, signage positioned
perpendicular to the path of travel is easiest for them to notice.
People can generally distinguish signage within an angle of 30
degrees to either side of the centerlines of their faces without
moving their heads.

A4.30.2 Character Proportion. The legibility of printed
characters is a function of the viewing distance, character height,
the ratio of the stroke width to the height of the character, the
contrast of color between character and background, and print
font. The size of characters must be based upon the intended
viewing distance. A severely nearsighted person may have to be
much closer to recognize a character of a given size than a
person with normal visual acuity.

**A4.30.4 Raised and Brailled Characters and Pictorial Symbol
Signs (Pictograms)**. The standard dimensions for literary Braille
are as follows:

Dot diameter	.059 in.
Inter-dot spacing	.090 in.
Horizontal separation between cells	.241 in.
Vertical separation between cells	.395 in.

Raised borders around signs containing raised characters may
make them confusing to read unless the border is set far away
from the characters. Accessible signage with descriptive
materials about public buildings, monuments, and objects of
cultural interest may not provide sufficiently detailed and
meaningful information. Interpretive guides, audio tape devices,
or other methods may be more effective in presenting such
information.

A4.30.5 Finish and Contrast. An eggshell finish (11 to 19
degree gloss on 60 degree glossimeter) is recommended.
Research indicates that signs are more legible for persons with

low vision when characters contrast with their background by at least 70 percent. Contrast in percent shall be determined by:

$$\text{Contrast} = [(B1 - B2)/B1] \times 100$$

where B1 = light reflectance value (LRV) of the lighter area and B2 = light reflectance value (LRV) of the darker area.

Note that in any application both white and black are never absolute; thus, B1 never equals 100 and B2 is always greater than 0.

The greatest readability is usually achieved through the use of light-colored characters or symbols on a dark background.

A4.30.7 Symbols of Accessibility for Different Types of Listening Systems. Paragraph 4 of this section requires signage indicating the availability of an assistive listening system. An appropriate message should be displayed with the international symbol of access for hearing loss since this symbol conveys general accessibility for people with hearing loss. Some suggestions are:

INFRARED
ASSISTIVE LISTENING SYSTEM
AVAILABLE
----PLEASE ASK----

AUDIO LOOP IN USE
TURN T-SWITCH FOR
BETTER HEARING
----OR ASK FOR HELP----

FM
ASSISTIVE LISTENING
SYSTEM AVAILABLE
----PLEASE ASK----

The symbol may be used to notify persons of the availability of other auxiliary aids and services such as: real time captioning, captioned note taking, sign language interpreters, and oral interpreters.

A4.30.8 Illumination Levels. Illumination levels on the sign surface shall be in the 100 to 300 lux range (10 to 30 footcandles) and shall be uniform over the sign surface. Signs shall be located such that the illumination level on the surface of the sign is not significantly exceeded by the ambient light or visible bright lighting source behind or in front of the sign.

A4.31 Telephones.

A4.31.3 Mounting Height. In localities where the dial-tone first system is in operation, calls can be placed at a coin telephone through the operator without inserting coins. The operator button is located at a height of 46 in (1170 mm) if the coin slot of the telephone is at 54 in (1370 mm). A generally available public telephone with a coin slot mounted lower on the equipment would allow universal installation of telephones at a height of 48 in (1220 mm) or less to all operable parts.
A4.31.9 Text Telephones. A public text telephone may be an

integrated text telephone pay phone unit or a conventional portable text telephone that is permanently affixed within, or adjacent to, the telephone enclosure. In order to be usable with a pay phone, a text telephone which is not a single integrated text telephone pay phone unit will require a shelf large enough (10 in (255mm) wide by 10 in (255 mm) deep with a 6 in (150 mm) vertical clearance minimum) to accommodate the device, an electrical outlet, and a power cord. Movable or portable text telephones may be used to provide equivalent facilitation. A text telephone should be readily available so that a person using it may access the text telephone easily and conveniently. As currently designed pocket-type text telephones for personal use do not accommodate a wide range of users. Such devices would not be considered substantially equivalent to conventional text telephones. However, in the future as technology develops this could change.

A4.32 Fixed or Built-in Seating and Tables.

A4.32.4 Height of Tables or Counters. Different types of work require different table or counter heights for comfort and optimal performance. Light detailed work such as writing requires a table or counter close to elbow height for a standing person. Heavy manual work such as rolling dough requires a counter or table height about 10 in (255 mm) below elbow height for a standing person. This principle of high/low table or counter heights also applies for seated persons; however, the limiting condition for seated manual work is clearance under the table or counter.

Table A1 shows convenient counter heights for seated persons. The great variety of heights for comfort and optimal performance indicates a need for alternatives or a compromise in height if people who stand and people who sit will be using the same counter area.

TABLE A1 CONVENIENT HEIGHTS OF TABLES AND COUNTERS FOR SEATED PEOPLE[1]

CONDITIONS OF USE	SHORT WOMEN in	mm	TALL MEN in	mm
Seated in a wheelchair: Manual work-				
Desk or removable armrests	26	660	30	760
Fixed, full-size armrests[2]	32[3]	815	32[3]	815
Light, detailed work: Desk or removable armrests	29	735	34	865
Fixed, full-size armrests[2]	32[3]	815	34	865
Seated in a 16 in (405 mm) High chair:				
Manual work	26	660	27	685
Light, detailed work	28	710	31	785

[1]All dimensions are based on a work-surface thickness of 1 1/2 in (38 mm) and a clearance of 1 1/2 in (38 mm) between legs and the underside of a work surface.

[2]This type of wheelchair arm does not interfere with the positioning of a wheelchair under a work surface.

[3]This dimension is limited by the height of the armrests: a lower height would be preferable. Some people in this group prefer lower work surfaces, which require positioning the wheelchair back from the edge of the counter.

A4.33 Assembly Areas.

A4.33.2 Size of Wheelchair Locations. Spaces large enough for two wheelchairs allow people who are coming to a performance together to sit together.

A4.33.3 Placement of Wheelchair Locations. The location of wheelchair areas can be planned so that a variety of positions within the seating area are provided. This will allow choice in viewing and price categories.

Building/life safety codes set minimum distances between rows of fixed seats with consideration of the number of seats in a row, the exit aisle width and arrangement, and the location of exit doors. "Continental" seating, with a greater number of seats per row and a commensurate increase in row spacing and exit doors, facilitates emergency egress for all people and increases ease of access to mid-row seats especially for people who walk with difficulty. Consideration of this positive attribute of "continental" seating should be included along with all other factors in the design of fixed seating areas.

A4.33.6 Placement of Listening Systems. A distance of 50 ft (15 m) allows a person to distinguish performers' facial expressions.

A4.33.7 Types of Listening Systems. An assistive listening system appropriate for an assembly area for a group of persons or where the specific individuals are not known in advance, such as a playhouse, lecture hall or movie theater, may be different from the system appropriate for a particular individual provided as an auxiliary aid or as part of a reasonable accommodation. The appropriate device for an individual is the type that individual can use, whereas the appropriate system for an assembly area will necessarily be geared toward the "average" or aggregate needs of various individuals. A listening system that can be used from any seat in a seating area is the most flexible way to meet this specification. Earphone jacks with variable volume controls can benefit only people who have slight hearing loss and do not help people who use hearing aids. At the present time, magnetic induction loops are the most feasible type of listening system for people who use hearing aids equipped with "T-coils," but people without hearing aids or those with hearing aids not equipped with inductive pick-ups cannot use them without special receivers. Radio frequency systems can be extremely effective and inexpensive. People without hearing aids can use them, but people with hearing aids need a special receiver to use them as they are presently designed. If hearing aids had a jack to allow a by-pass of microphones, then radio frequency systems would be suitable for people with and without hearing aids. Some listening systems may be subject to interference from other equipment and feedback from hearing aids of people who are using the systems. Such interference can be controlled by careful engineering design that anticipates feedback sources in the surrounding area.

Table A2, reprinted from a National Institute of Disability and Rehabilitation Research "Rehab Brief," shows some of the advantages and disadvantages of different types of assistive listening systems. In addition, the Architectural and Transportation Barriers Compliance Board (Access Board) has published a pamphlet on Assistive Listening Systems which lists demonstration centers across the country where technical assistance can be obtained in selecting and installing appropriate systems. The state of New York has also adopted a detailed technical specification which may be useful.

Table A2. Summary of Assistive Listening Devices

Induction Loop

Transmitter: Transducer wired to induction loop around listening area.
Receiver: Self-contained induction receiver or personal hearing aid with telecoil.

Advantages

Cost -Effective
Low Maintenance
Easy to use
Unobtrusive
May be possible to integrate into existing public address system.
Some hearing aids can function as receivers.

Disadvantages

Signal spills over to adjacent rooms.
Susceptible to electrical interference.
Limited portability
Inconsistent signal strength
Head position affects signal strength.
Lack of standards for induction coil performance.
Typical Applications

Meeting areas
Theaters
Churches and Temples
Conference rooms
Classrooms
TV viewing

FM

Transmitter: Flashlight-sized worn by speaker.
Receiver: With personal hearing aid via DAI or induction neck-loop and telecoil; or self-contained with earphone(s).

Advantages

Highly portable
Different channels allow use by different groups within the same room.
High user mobility
Variable for large range of hearing losses.

Disadvantages

High cost of receivers
Equipment fragile
Equipment obtrusive
High maintenance
Expensive to maintain
Custom fitting to individual user may be required.

Typical Applications

Classrooms
Tour groups
Meeting areas
Outdoor events
One-on-one

Infrared

Transmitter: Emitter in line-of- sight with receiver.
Receiver: Self-contained. Or with personal hearing aid via DAI or induction neckloop and telecoil.

Advantages

Easy to use
Insures privacy or confidentiality
Moderate cost
Can often be integrated into existing public address system.

Disadvantages

Line-of-sight required between emitter and receiver.
Ineffective outdoors
Limited portability
Requires installation

Typical Applications

Theaters
Churches and Temples
Auditoriums Meetings requiring confidentiality
TV viewing

Source: Rehab Brief, National Institute on Disability and Rehabilitation Research, Washington, DC, Vol. XII, No. 10, (1990).

A5.0 Restaurants and Cafeterias.

A5.1 General. Dining counters (where there is no service) are typically found in small carry-out restaurants, bakeries, or coffee shops and may only be a narrow eating surface attached to a wall. This section requires that where such a dining counter is provided, a portion of the counter shall be at the required accessible height.

A7.0 Business and Mercantile.

A7.2(3) Assistive Listening Devices. At all sales and service counters, teller windows, box offices, and information kiosks where a physical barrier separates service personnel and customers, it is recommended that at least one permanently installed assistive listening device complying with 4.33 be provided at each location or series. Where assistive listening devices are installed, signage should be provided identifying those stations which are so equipped.

A7.3 Check-Out Aisles. Section 7.2 refers to counters without aisles; section 7.3 concerns check-out aisles. A counter without an aisle (7.2) can be approached from more than one direction such as in a convenience store. In order to use a check-out aisle (7.3), customers must enter a defined area (an aisle) at a particular point, pay for goods, and exit at a particular point.

A10.3 Fixed Facilities and Stations.

A10.3.1(7) Route Signs. One means of making control buttons on fare vending machines usable by persons with vision impairments is to raise them above the surrounding surface. Those activated by a mechanical motion are likely to be more detectable. If farecard vending, collection, and adjustment devices are designated to accommodate farecards having one tactually distinctive corner, then a person who has a vision impairment will insert the card with greater ease. Token collection devices that are designed to accommodate tokens which are perforated can allow a person to distinguish more readily between tokens and common coins. Thoughtful placement of accessible gates and fare vending machines in relation to inaccessible devices will make their use and detection easier for all persons with disabilities.

Table 1
Graphic Conventions

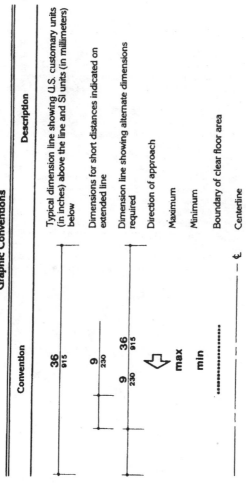

Convention	Description
36 / 915	Typical dimension line showing U.S. customary units (in inches) above the line and SI units (in millimeters) below
9 / 230	Dimensions for short distances indicated on extended line
9 230 / **36** 915	Dimension line showing alternate dimensions required
⇩	Direction of approach
max	Maximum
min	Minimum
▪▪▪▪▪▪▪▪▪	Boundary of clear floor area
— · — ₵	Centerline

(**EDITOR'S NOTE:** Limited editor's notes have been added to these ADAAG figures to provide clarification and assistance to Pocket Guide Users. These notes are the opinions of the editor and not official interpretations.)

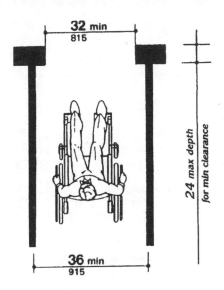

Fig. 1
Minimum Clear Width
for Single Wheelchair

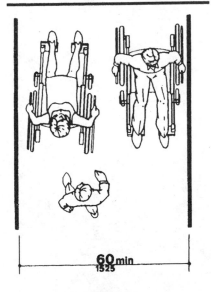

Fig. 2
Minimum Clear Width
for Two Wheelchairs

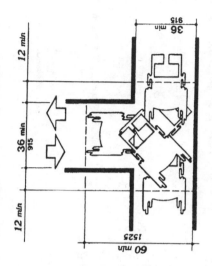

(b)
T-Shaped Space for 180° Turns

Fig. 3
Wheelchair Turning Space

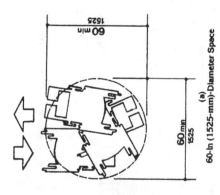

(a)
60-in (1525-mm)-Diameter Space

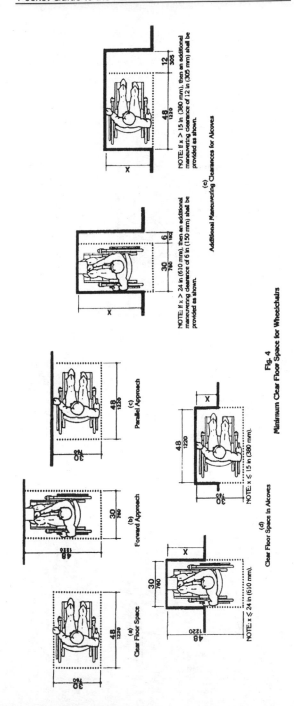

Fig. 4
Minimum Clear Floor Space for Wheelchairs

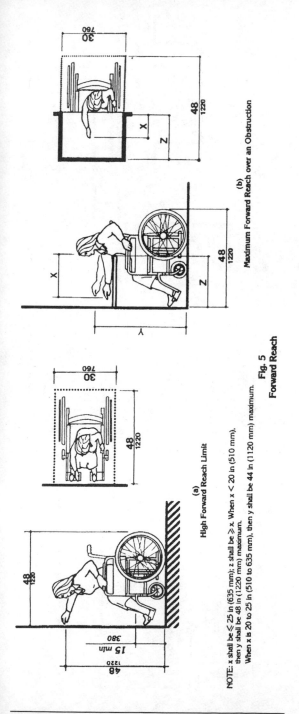

(a)

High Forward Reach Limit

(b)

Maximum Forward Reach over an Obstruction

NOTE: x shall be ≤ 25 in (635 mm); z shall be ≥ x. When x < 20 in (510 mm), then y shall be 48 in (1220 mm) maximum. When x is 20 to 25 in (510 to 635 mm), then y shall be 44 in (1120 mm) maximum.

Fig. 5
Forward Reach

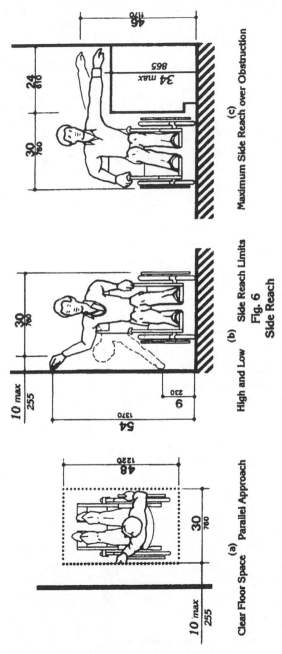

(a) Clear Floor Space   Parallel Approach

(b) High and Low   Side Reach Limits

(c) Maximum Side Reach over Obstruction

Fig. 6
Side Reach

(**EDITOR'S NOTE**: See section 4.34.3(2)(b) for additional options.)

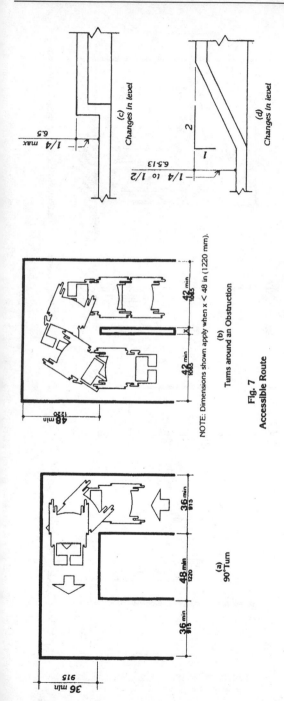

(c) Changes in level

6.5 — 1/4 max

(d) Changes in level

6.5-13 — 1/4 to 1/2

NOTE: Dimensions shown apply when x < 48 in (1220 mm).

(b) Turns around an Obstruction

42 min 1065   X   42 min 1065

48 min 1250

Fig. 7
Accessible Route

(a) 90° Turn

36 min 915   48 min 1220   36 min 915

36 min 915

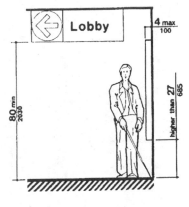

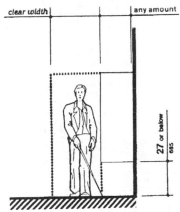

Fig. 8 (a)
Walking Parallel to a Wall

Fig. 8 (b)
Walking Perpendicular to a Wall

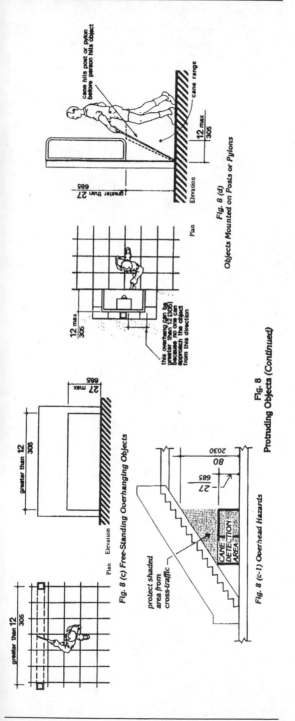

Fig. 8 (d)
Objects Mounted on Posts or Pylons

Fig. 8 (c) Free-Standing Overhanging Objects

Fig. 8
Protruding Objects (Continued)

Fig. 8 (c-1) Overhead Hazards

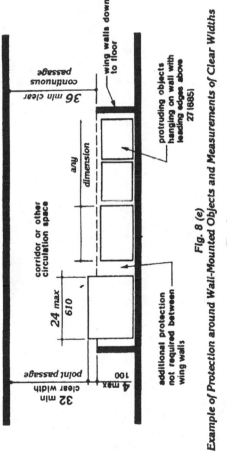

Fig. 8 (e)
Example of Protection around Wall-Mounted Objects and Measurements of Clear Widths

Fig. 8
Protruding Objects (Continued)

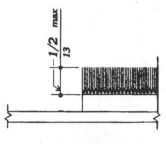

Fig. 8 (f)
Carpet Pile Thickness

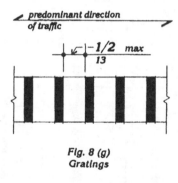

Fig. 8 (g)
Gratings

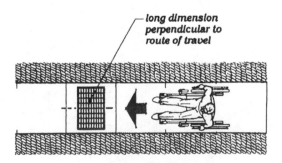

Fig. 8 (h)
Grating Orientation

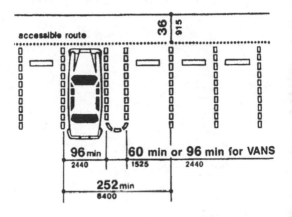

Fig. 9
Dimensions of Parking Spaces

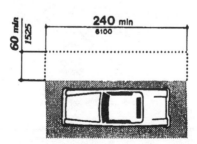

Fig. 10
Access Aisle at Passenger Loading Zones

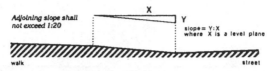

Fig. 11
Measurement of Curb Ramp Slopes

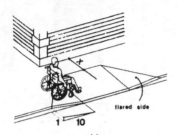

(a)
Flared Sides

If X is less than 48 in,
then the slope of the flared side
shall not exceed 1:12.

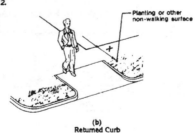

(b)
Returned Curb

Fig. 12
Sides of Curb Ramps

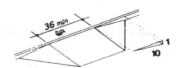

Fig. 13
Built-Up Curb Ramp

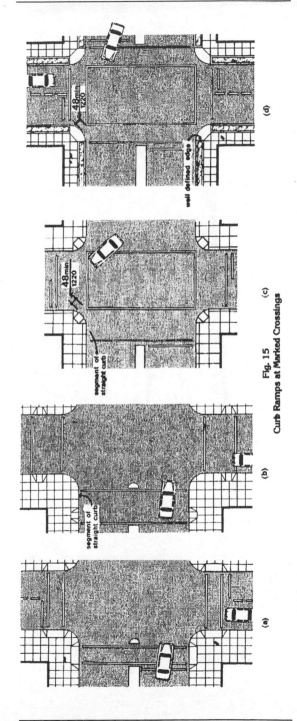

**Fig. 15
Curb Ramps at Marked Crossings**

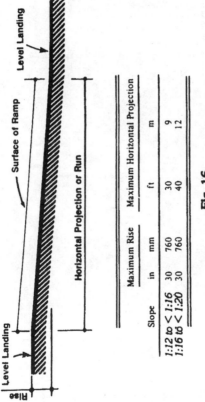

Slope	Maximum Rise		Maximum Horizontal Projection	
	in	mm	ft	m
1:12 to < 1:16	30	760	30	9
1:16 to < 1:20	30	760	40	12

Fig. 16

Components of a Single Ramp Run and Sample Ramp Dimensions

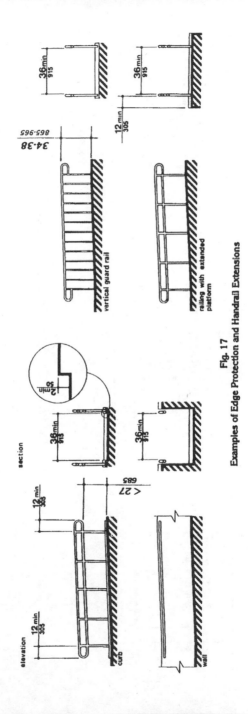

Fig. 17
Examples of Edge Protection and Handrail Extensions

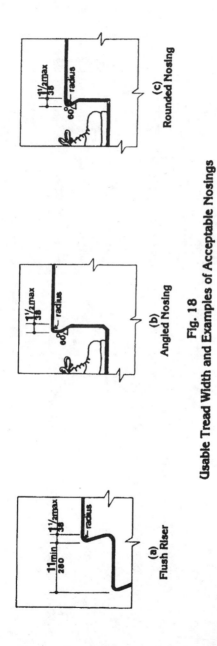

Fig. 18
Usable Tread Width and Examples of Acceptable Nosings

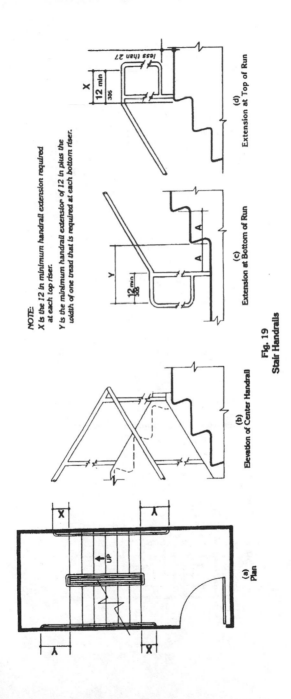

NOTE:
X is the 12 in minimum handrail extension required at each top riser.

Y is the minimum handrail extension of 12 in plus the width of one tread that is required at each bottom riser.

(a)
Plan

(b)
Elevation of Center Handrail

(c)
Extension at Bottom of Run

12 min
305

(d)
Extension at Top of Run

12 min
305

less than 27

Fig. 19
Stair Handrails

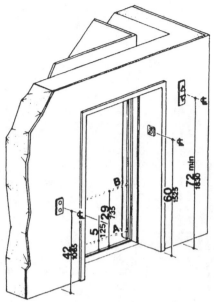

NOTE: The automatic door reopening device is activated if an object passes through either line A or line B. Line A and line B represent the vertical locations of the door reopening device not requiring contact.

Fig. 20
Hoistway and Elevator Entrances

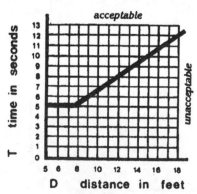

Fig. 21
Graph of Timing Equation

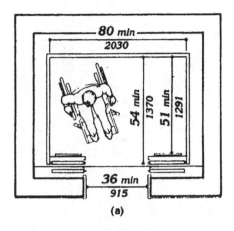

(a)

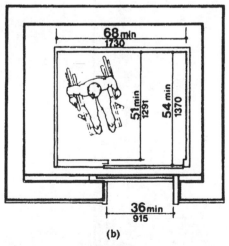

(b)

Fig. 22
Minimum Dimensions of Elevator Cars

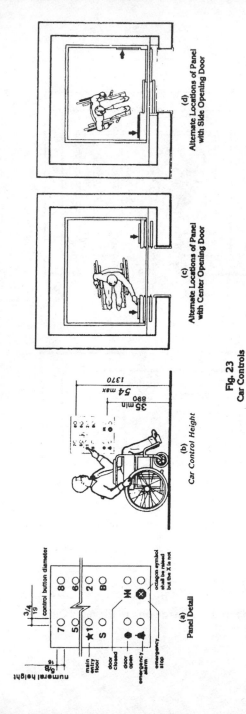

(a) Panel Detail

(b) Car Control Height

(c) Alternate Locations of Panel with Center Opening Door

(d) Alternate Locations of Panel with Side Opening Door

**Fig. 23
Car Controls**

(EDITOR'S NOTE: In fig. 23(b), 54" max. control Ht. is for side approach only. Forward approach max. Ht. is 48" per 4.10.12(3).)

106

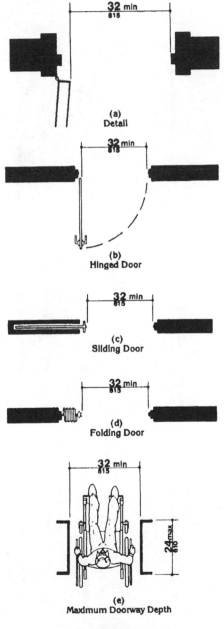

(a)
Detail

(b)
Hinged Door

(c)
Sliding Door

(d)
Folding Door

(e)
Maximum Doorway Depth

Fig. 24
Clear Doorway Width and Depth

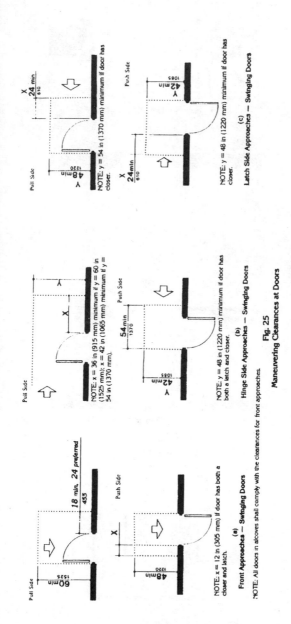

NOTE: x = 12 in (305 mm) if door has both a closer and latch.

(a)
Front Approaches — Swinging Doors

NOTE: x = 36 in (915 mm) minimum if y = 60 in (1525 mm); x = 42 in (1065 mm) minimum if y = 54 in (1370 mm).

NOTE: y = 48 in (1220 mm) minimum if door has both a latch and closer.

(b)
Hinge Side Approaches — Swinging Doors

NOTE: y = 54 in (1370 mm) minimum if door has closer.

NOTE: y = 48 in (1220 mm) minimum if door has closer.

(c)
Latch Side Approaches — Swinging Doors

Fig. 25
Maneuvering Clearances at Doors

NOTE: All doors in alcoves shall comply with the clearances for front approaches.

108

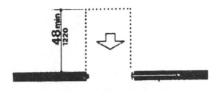

(d)
Front Approach — Sliding Doors
and Folding Doors

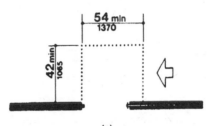

(e)
Slide Side Approach — Sliding Doors
and Folding Doors

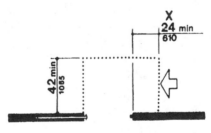

(f)
Latch Side Approach — Sliding Doors *and Folding Doors*

NOTE: All doors in alcoves shall comply with the
clearances for front approaches.

Fig. 25
Maneuvering Clearances at Doors *(Continued)*

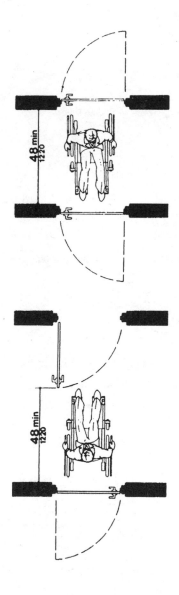

Fig. 26
Two Hinged Doors in Series

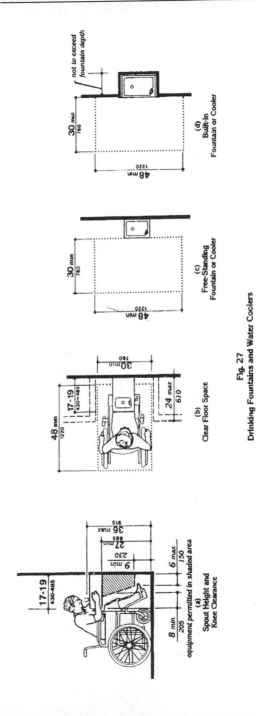

Fig. 27
Drinking Fountains and Water Coolers

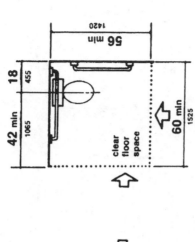

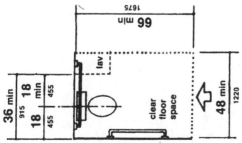

Fig. 28
Clear Floor Space at Water Closets

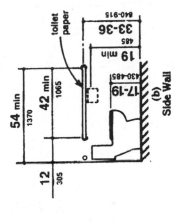

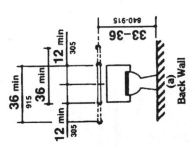

Fig. 29
Grab Bars at Water Closets

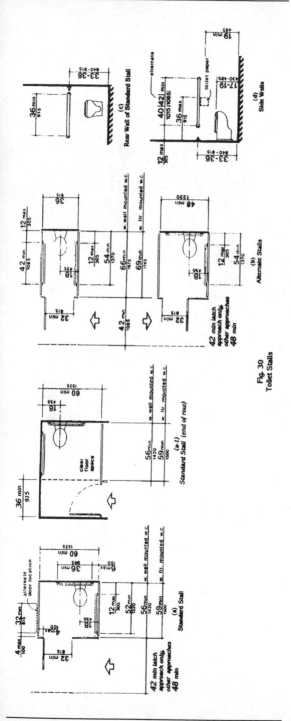

Fig. 30
Toilet Stalls

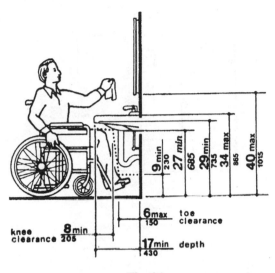

**Fig. 31
Lavatory Clearances**

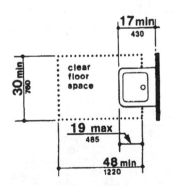

**Fig. 32
Clear Floor Space at Lavatories**

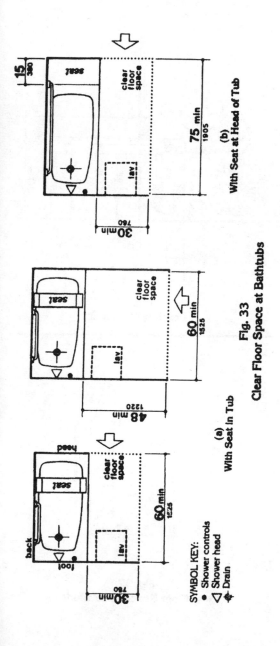

SYMBOL KEY:
- Shower controls
- ▽ Shower head
- Drain

(a)
With Seat in Tub

(b)
With Seat at Head of Tub

Fig. 33
Clear Floor Space at Bathtubs

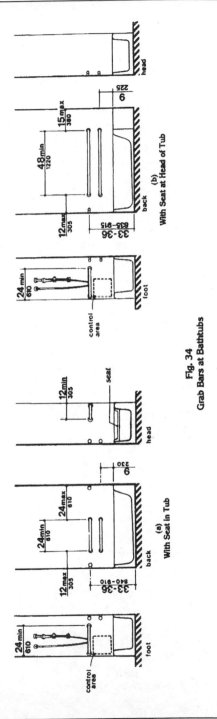

Fig. 34
Grab Bars at Bathtubs

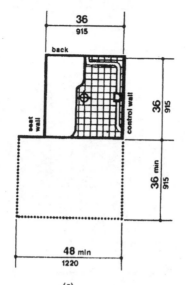

(a)
36·in by 36·in
(915·mm by 915·mm) Stall

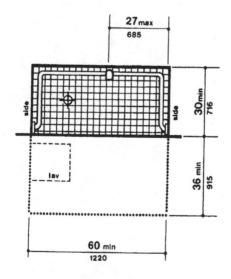

(b)
30·in by 60·in
(760·mm by 1525·mm) Stall

Fig. 35
Shower Size and Clearances

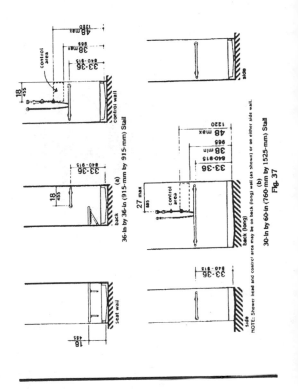

36-in by 36-in (915-mm by 915-mm) Stall
(a)

30-in by 60-in (760-mm by 1525-mm) Stall
(b)

NOTE: Shower head and control area may be on back (long) wall (as shown) or on either side wall.

Fig. 37

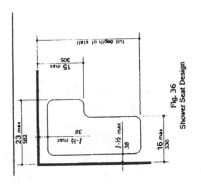

Fig. 36
Shower Seat Design

(**EDITOR'S NOTE:** Seat height is 17"-19" (not limited to 18") per 4.21.3.)

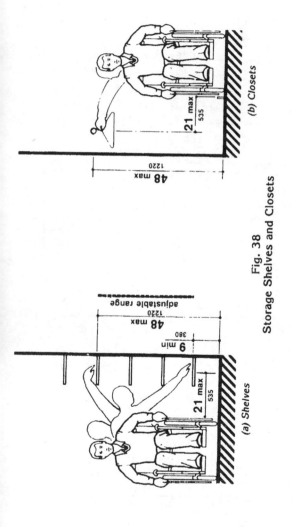

(a) Shelves

(b) Closets

Fig. 38
Storage Shelves and Closets

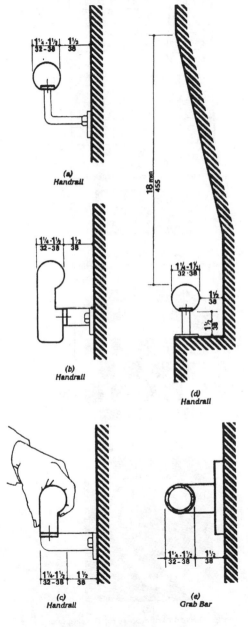

Fig. 39
Size and Spacing of Handrails and Grab Bars

(a)
Proportions
International Symbol of Accessibility

(b)
Display Conditions
International Symbol of Accessibility

(c)
International TDD Symbol

(d)
International Symbol of Access for Hearing Loss

Fig. 43
International Symbols

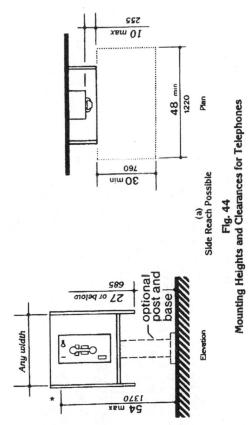

(a)
Side Reach Possible

Fig. 44
Mounting Heights and Clearances for Telephones

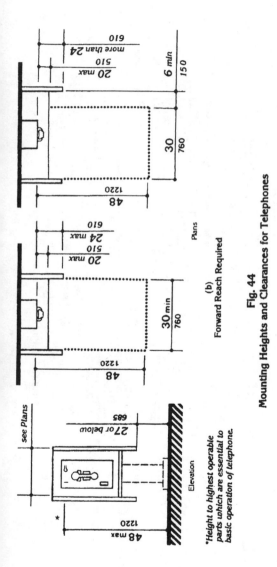

Plans

**(b)
Forward Reach Required**

Elevation

Height to highest operable parts which are essential to basic operation of telephone.

**Fig. 44
Mounting Heights and Clearances for Telephones**

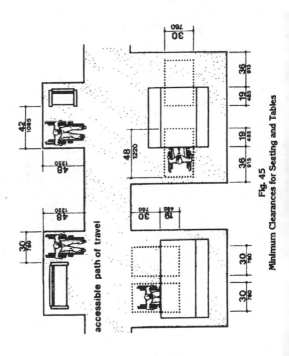

Fig. 45
Minimum Clearances for Seating and Tables

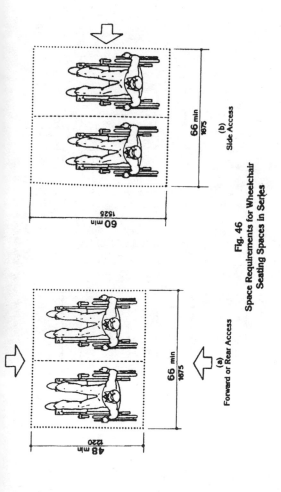

Fig. 46
Space Requirements for Wheelchair
Seating Spaces in Series

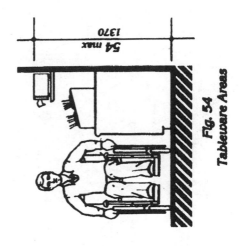

**Fig. 54
Tableware Areas**

54 max
1370

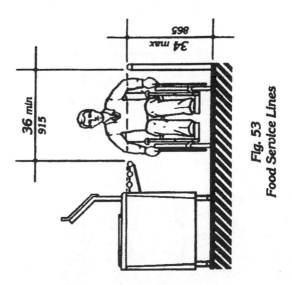

**Fig. 53
Food Service Lines**

34 max
865

36 min
915

(**EDITOR'S NOTE**: See 4.34.3(2)(b) for tableware and condiment reach limits.)

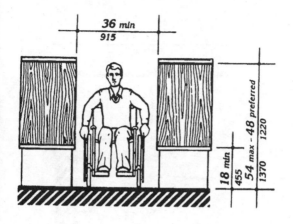

Fig. 55
Card Catalog

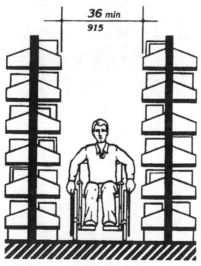

Fig. 56
Stacks

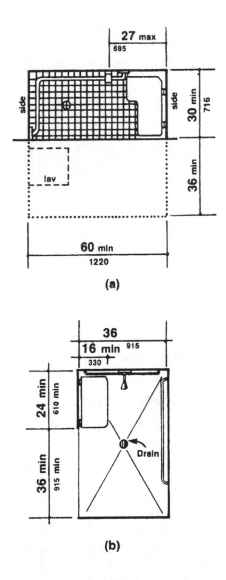

(a)

(b)

Fig. 57
Roll-in Shower with Folding Seat

(**EDITOR'S NOTE:** Fig. 57(b) may provide the best options for the greatest number of users as transfer or roll-in shower.)

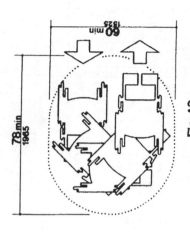

Fig. A2
Space Needed for Smooth U-Turn in a Wheelchair

Fig. A1
**Minimum Passage Width for One Wheelchair
and One Ambulatory Person**

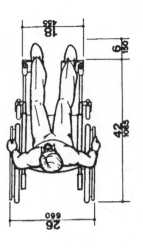

NOTE: Footrests may extend further for tall people

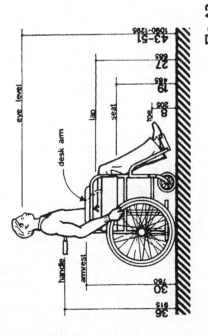

Fig. A3
Dimensions of Adult-Sized Wheelchairs

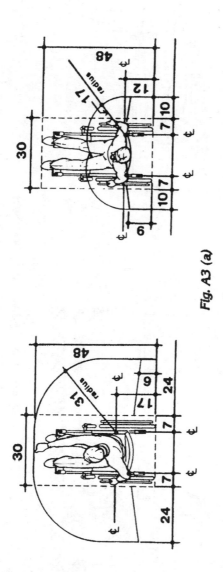

Fig. A3 (a)

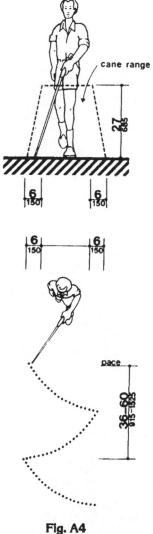

cane range

27
685

6
150

6
150

6
150

6
150

pace

36-60
915-1525

Fig. A4
Cane Technique

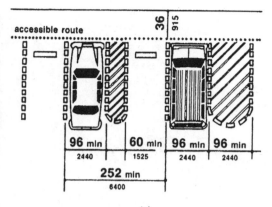

(a)
Van Accessible Space at End Row

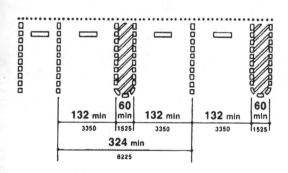

(b)
Universal Parking Space Design

Fig. A5
Parking Space Alternatives

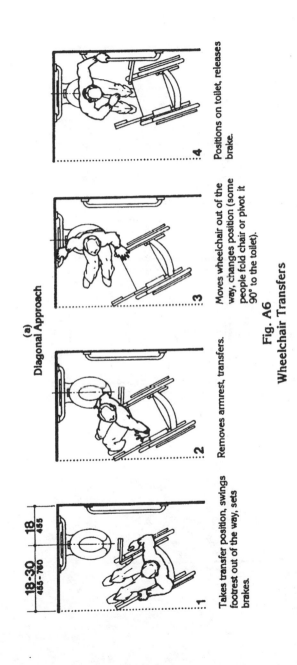

(a)
Diagonal Approach

1. Takes transfer position, swings footrest out of the way, sets brakes.

2. Removes armrest, transfers.

3. Moves wheelchair out of the way, changes position (some people fold chair or pivot it 90° to the toilet).

4. Positions on toilet, releases brake.

Fig. A6
Wheelchair Transfers

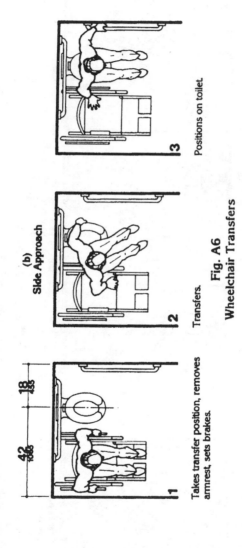

(b)
Side Approach

Fig. A6
Wheelchair Transfers

1. Takes transfer position, removes armrest, sets brakes.
2. Transfers.
3. Positions on toilet.

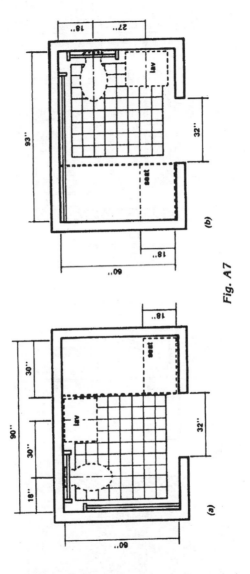

Fig. A7

(**EDITOR'S NOTE:** These conceptual diagrams only apply when roll-in shower is used. These drawings show non-compliant grab bars and omit many requirements. See A4.23.3)

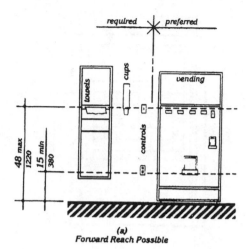

(a)
Forward Reach Possible

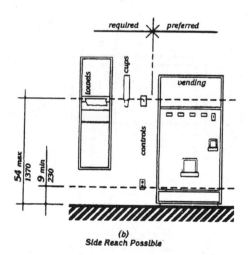

(b)
Side Reach Possible

Fig. A8
Control Reach Limitations

(**EDITOR'S NOTE:** Electrical outlet shown in fig. A8(b) is not necessarily compliant with 4.27.3.)